Also by David DeFord

Ordinary People Can Achieve Their Lofty Goals

1000 Brilliant Achievement Quotes: Wisdom from the World's Wisest

Ordinary People Can Achieve the Extraordinary: A Practical Guide to Goal Achievement

I Wish to Be Useful: A Guide for More Meaningful Living

Where Seldom Is Heard a Discouraging Word: Encouragement for Successful and Meaningful Living

Make Your Life a Masterpiece

Good News about Business Networking

Hippie Serendipity: A Story of Peace, Love, and Freedom

**Available at
http://daviddeford.com/ddblog/books/**

1000 Brilliant Leadership Quotes

Advice from the World's Wisest Leaders

David DeFord

Ordinary People Can Win!
Omaha, NE

Copyright © 2004, 2018 David DeFord and Ordinary People Can Win!
All Rights Reserved.
ISBN 978-1985197022

David DeFord Creative Consulting 13964 Margo Street
Omaha, NE 68138
david@daviddeford.com

David DeFord is dedicated to helping his clients and audience members to dig their work.

David's blog, DavidDeFord.com, provides regular updates on job satisfaction tips.

To book David for your convention or annual meeting, e-mail him at **david@daviddeford.com**.

You can find the author on the following social media:
LinkedIn: LinkedIn.com/in/daviddeford
Twitter: @DavidDeFord

David DeFord is dedicated to helping people dig their work.

According to multiple studies, more than 60% of people are unhappy at their work. They dream of changing jobs, starting their own company, or retiring to leisure pursuit.

More than 90% complain about their work more than ten times a day.

Is that you?

I propose you quit griping and do something. I can help.

Coaching: Through coaching I can help you take actions that will lead you to better satisfaction.

Training: I can train your organization, your executives, or your whole leadership team to improve the job satisfaction and productivity at your organization.

Speaking: Bring me in to speak to your teams at your annual meetings or at your association conferences. You will help your people lift their vision from what they don't like at work to what they can do about their complaints.

About the Author

David DeFord has studied personal development all of his adult life. Having discovered Dale Carnegie, Napoleon Hill, and Dr. Norman Vincent Peale as a young man, he has read and put into practice many of the teachings of the greatest motivational teachers of our time.

A frequent and popular speaker, he has honed his talents over the years. He's spoken to more than 1300 audiences in all 50 states and across Canada. His enthusiasm and passion lifts his audiences.

A long-time information technology executive, David has served as manager, director, vice president, and officer of regional corporations.

David has been married to the love of his life, Kathy, since 1972. They have four children, and several grandchildren. They actively participate in church and volunteer organizations.

Table of Contents

Introduction	1
The Need for Leaders	3
Leaders Have Vision	6
Change and Innovation	18
Greatness	26
The Leader as Servant	37
Integrity	42
A Leader Motivates	54
Build Future Leaders	59
Respect for Associates	66
Communication Travels Both Ways	71
Courage to Seize Opportunities	78
Teamwork	99
Confidence	107
Decisiveness	109
Determination	117
Excellence	120
Focus	131
Growth and Learning	133
Persuasion and Communication	137
Planning and Preparation	152
Sources	154

Introduction

Dream Big and Dare to Fail

Let me introduce a man who lived by the motto, "dream big and dare to fail."

Norman Vaughan recently died a few days after his 100th birthday.

Vaughan served as dog handler and driver in Admiral Richard Byrd's expedition to the South Pole in 1928. He drove the dog teams 1,500 miles across Antarctica to collect scientific data.

Just a few days before his 89th birthday, Vaughan and his wife returned to Antarctica and climbed to the top of 10,320-foot Mount Vaughan, the mountain named in his honor.

Norman Vaughan sought adventure all his life.

He finished the 1,100 mile Iditarod Trail Sled Dog Race six times after age 70. At age 96 he carried the Olympic Torch—70 years after he competed in the Olympic Games as a sled dog racer.

Vaughan planned to climb Mount Vaughan again to celebrate his 100th birthday, but his funding fell short.

He wrote two books, "With Byrd at the Bottom of the World," the story of his South Pole adventure, and "My Life of Adventure," about his other exploits.

Norman Vaughan lived his motto, "dream big and dare to fail" for 100 years.

You may not drive a dog team across Antarctica, but you can dream big and dare to fail.

Most big dreams have associated risks. And many people trade their big dreams for comfort and safety.

Don't trade away your dreams for a little comfort. Have you have always swallowed your big dreams—afraid to put your lesser attainments at risk?

I challenge you to count the cost of chasing your dreams and compare that cost against living a life far short of them.

You will not succeed every step of the way. You will suffer some losses. You will fail to meet your expectations at times. But if you plan, and work, and strive toward your dreams, you will attain them.

You can do this.

Dream big and dare to fail.

Chapter 1

The Need for Leaders

The quality of leadership, more than any other single factor, determines the success or failure of an organization.
Fred Fiedler & Martin Chemers

Great necessities call forth great leaders.
Abigail Adams

The only safe ship in a storm is leadership.
Faye Wattleton

Men make history and not the other way around. In periods where there is no leadership, society stands still. Progress occurs when courageous, skillful leaders seize the opportunity to change things for the better.
Harry S Truman

No organization is stronger than the quality of its leadership, or ever extends its constituency far beyond the degree to which its leadership is representative.
Edgar Powell

The quality of leadership, more than any other single factor, determines the success or failure of an organization.
Fred Fiedler and Martin Chemers

Inspired leaders move a business beyond problems into opportunities.
Dr. Abraham Zaleznik

Leadership happens at every level of the organization and no one can shirk from this responsibility.
Jerry Junkins

There are many elements to a campaign. Leadership is number one. Everything else is number two.
Bernd Brecher

All nations seek it constantly because it is the key to greatness, sometimes to survival . . . the electric and the elusive quality known as leadership.
General Mark W. Clark

I am personally convinced that one person can be a change catalyst, a transformer in any situation, any organization. Such an individual is yeast that can leaven an entire loaf. It requires vision, initiative, patience, respect, persistence, courage, and faith to be a transforming leader.
Stephen R. Covey

Men make history, and not the other way around. In periods where there is no leadership, society stands still. Progress occurs when courageous, skillful leaders seize the opportunity to change things for the better.
Harry S Truman

Chapter 2

Great Leaders Have Vision

The very essence of leadership is that you have to have vision. You can't blow an uncertain trumpet.
Theodore Hesburgh

The first responsibility of a leader is to define reality. The last is to say thank you.
Max DePree

A new leader has to be able to change an organization that is dreamless, soulless and visionless ... someone's got to make a wake up call.
Warren Bennis

Where there is no vision, the people perish.
Proverbs 29:18

The very essence of leadership is its purpose. And the purpose of leadership is to accomplish a task. That is what leadership does--and what it does is more important than what it is or how it works.
Colonel Dandridge M. Malone

We know not where our dreams will take us, but we can probably see quite clearly where we'll go without them.
Marilyn Grey

Don't be afraid of the space between your dreams and reality. If you can dream it you can make it so.
Belva Davis

Leadership can be thought of as a capacity to define oneself to others in a way that clarifies and expands a vision of the future.
Edwin H. Friedman

If I have seen farther than others, it is because I was standing on the shoulder of giants.
Isaac Newton

The very essence of leadership is that you have to have a vision.
Theodore Hesburgh

To the person who does not know where he wants to go there is no favorable wind.
Seneca

A leader has the vision and conviction that a dream can be achieved. He inspires the power and energy to get it done.
Ralph Lauren

A leader's role is to raise people's aspirations for what they can become and to release their energies so they will try to get there.
David Gergen

Destiny is not a matter of chance, but of choice. Not something to wish for, but to attain.
William Jennings Bryan

Dream lofty dreams, and as you dream, so shall you become. Your Vision is the promise of what you shall one day be. Your Ideal is the prophecy of what you shall at last unveil.
James Allen

Big thinking precedes great achievement.
Wilferd Peterson

The future belongs to those who see possibilities before they become obvious.
John Scully

If one advances confidently in the direction of his dreams, and endeavors to live the life which he has imagined, he will meet with success unexpected in common hours.
Henry David Thoreau

If you limit your choices only to what seems possible or reasonable, you disconnect yourself from what you truly want, and all that is left is a compromise.
Robert Fritz

Vision is the art of seeing the invisible.
Jonathan Swift

It is very dangerous to go into eternity with possibilities which one has oneself prevented from becoming realities. A possibility is a hint from God. One must follow it.
Sören Kierkegaard

Create your future from your future, not your past.
Werner Erhard

Looking up gives light, although at first it makes you dizzy.
Mevlana Rumi

No matter how dark things seem to be or actually are, raise your sights and see the possibilities – always see them, for they're always there.
Norman Vincent Peale

Nothing stops an organization faster than people who believe that the way you worked yesterday is the best way to work tomorrow.
Jon Madonna

To grasp and hold a vision, that is the very essence of successful leadership—not only on the movie set where I learned it, but everywhere.
Ronald Reagan

You've got to think about big things while you're doing small things, so that all the small things go in the right direction.
Alvin Toffler

Leadership is the capacity to translate vision into reality.
Warren Bennis

You want to set a goal that is big enough that in the process of achieving it you become someone worth becoming.
Jim Rohn

Common sense is the knack of seeing things as they are, and doing things as they ought to be done.
Harriet Beecher Stowe

The greatest danger for most of us is not that our aim is too high and we miss it, but that it is too low and we reach it.
Michelangelo

If you want to be happy, set a goal that commands your thoughts, liberates your energy, and inspires your hopes.
Andrew Carnegie

If you are bored with life, if you don't get up every morning with a burning desire to do things—you don't have enough goals.
Lou Holtz

Dreams are extremely important. You can't do it unless you can imagine it.
George Lucas

Peak performers want more than merely to win the next game. They see all the way to the championship. They have a long-range goal that inspires commitment and action.
Charles Garfield

Achievement is largely the product of steadily raising one's levels of aspiration and expectation.
Jack Nicklaus

Celebrate what you've accomplished, but raise the bar a little higher each time you succeed.
Mia Hamm

In the long run men hit only what they aim at.
Henry David Thoreau

So many of our dreams seem impossible, then improbable, then inevitable.
Christopher Reeve

There is no more powerful engine driving an organization toward excellence and long-range success than an attractive, worthwhile, achievable vision for the future, widely shared.
Burt Nanus

If you want to build a ship, don't herd people together to collect wood and don't assign them tasks and work, but rather teach them to long for the endless immensity of the sea.
Antoine de Saint-Exupery

Let's make a dent in the universe.
Steve Jobs

The vision must be followed by the venture. It is not enough to stare up the steps - we must step up the stairs.
Vance Havne

Do not follow where the path may lead. Go instead where there is no path and leave a trail.
Harold R. McAlindon

A leader is one who knows the way, goes the way, and shows the way.
John C. Maxwell

People buy into the leader before they buy into the vision.
John C. Maxwell

If your actions inspire others to dream more, learn more, do more and become more, you are a leader.
John Quincy Adams

Leadership is practiced not so much in words as in attitude and in actions.
Harold S. Geneen

You read a book from beginning to end. You run a business the opposite way. You start with the end, and then you do everything you must to reach it.
Harold S. Geneen

We may be very busy, we may be very efficient, but we will also be truly effective only when we begin with the end in mind.
Stephen R. Covey

The main thing is to keep the main thing the main thing.
Stephen R. Covey

Leaders must invoke an alchemy of great vision.
Henry Kissinger

There is no passion to be found in playing small – in settling for a life that is less than what you are capable of living.
Nelson Mandela

A leader has the vision and conviction that a dream can be achieved. He inspires the power and energy to get it done.
Ralph Nader

The very essence of leadership is [that] you have a vision. It's got to be a vision you articulate clearly and forcefully on every occasion. You can't blow an uncertain trumpet.
Theodore Hesburgh

Leadership is the special quality which enables people to stand up and pull the rest of us over the horizon.
James L. Fisher

A frightened captain makes a frightened crew.
Lister Sinclair

The nation will find it very hard to look up to the leaders who are keeping their ears to the ground.
Winston Churchill

The size of a leader is determined by the depth of his convictions, the height of his ambitions, the breadth of his vision and the reach of his love.
D. N. Jackson

People learn to lead because they care about something.
Charlotte Bunch

We need women leaders. But we need them to have a vision for something.
Charlotte Bunch

Every successful leader must instill the vision of where the organization is going and what is necessary to attain that goal.
John Di Frances

The six essential leadership attributes: set high standards; live your standards and mentor those who follow; create and share a vision; make the hard choices when necessary; be visible and out front; and instill hope in those who follow.
John Di Frances

Leaders can conceive and articulate goals that lift people out of their petty preoccupations and unite them in pursuit of objectives worthy of their best efforts.
John William Gardner

A great leader's courage to fulfill his vision comes from passion, not position.
John C. Maxwell

Where there is no hope in the future, there is no power in the present.
John C. Maxwell

Cherish your visions and your dreams as they are the children of your soul; the blueprints of your ultimate achievements.
Napoleon Hill

As long as you're going to be thinking anyway, you might as well think big.
Donald Trump

Twenty years from now you will be more disappointed by the things you didn't do than by the ones you did do. So throw off the bowlines, sail away from the safe harbor. Catch the trade winds in your sails. Explore. Dream. Discover.
Mark Twain

It's easy to count the seeds in an apple, but only God can count the apples in a single seed.
Dr. Robert Schuller

He who has a why to live for can bear almost any how.
Friedrich Nietzsche

The ripest peach is highest on the tree.
James Whitcomb Riley

Determine what specific goal you want to achieve. Then dedicate yourself to its attainment with unswerving singleness of purpose, the trenchant zeal of a crusader.
Paul J. Meyer

You will become as great as your dominant aspiration. If you cherish a vision, a lofty ideal in your heart, you will realize it.
James Allen

There is one quality which one must possess to win, and that is definiteness of purpose, the knowledge of what one wants and a burning desire to possess it.
Ronald Reagan

Visualize this thing you want. See it, feel it, believe in it. Make your mental blueprint and begin.
Robert Collier

Leadership is not magnetic personality - that can just as well be a glib tongue. It is not making friends and influencing people -- that is flattery. Leadership is lifting a person's vision to high sights, the raising of a person's performance to a higher standard, the building of a personality beyond its normal limitations.
Peter Drucker

The leader has to be practical and a realist, yet must talk the language of the visionary and the idealist.
Eric Hoffer

Chapter 3

Change and Innovation

I used to think that running an organization was equivalent to conducting a symphony orchestra. But I don't think that's quite it; it's more like jazz. There is more improvisation.
Warren Bennis

Do not follow where the path may lead. Go instead where there is no path and leave a trail.
Muriel Strode

The leader has to be practical and a realist, yet must talk the language of the visionary and the idealist.
Eric Hoffer

The significant problems we face cannot be solved at the same level of thinking we were at when we created them.
Albert Einstein

When we think of leaders, we remember times of change, innovation and conflict.
Charles E. Rice

There is nothing more difficult to take in hand, more perilous to conduct, or more uncertain in its success, than to take the lead in the introduction of a new order of things.
Niccolo Machiavelli

The rate of change is not going to slow down anytime soon. If anything, competition in most industries will probably speed up even more in the next few decades.
John P. Kotter

People don't resist change. They resist being changed!
Peter Senge

Your success in life isn't based on your ability to simply change. It is based on your ability to change faster than your competition, customers and business.
Mark Sanborn

The most successful businessman is the man who holds onto the old just as long as it is good, and grabs the new just as soon as it is better.
Robert P. Vanderpoel

As the births of living creatures are at first ill-shapen, so are all innovations, which are the births of time.
Francis Bacon

Never doubt that a small group of thoughtful, concerned citizens can change the world. Indeed it is the only thing that ever has.
Margaret Mead

I'll go anywhere as long as it's forward.
David Livingstone

Ten years ago, Peter Senge introduced the idea of the 'learning organization' Now he says that for big companies to change, we need to stop thinking like mechanics and to start acting like gardeners.
Alan M. Webber

Capital isn't so important in business. Experience isn't so important. You can get both these things. What is important is ideas. If you have ideas, you have the main asset you need, and there isn't any limit to what you can do with your business and your life.
Harvey Firestone

Creativity, as has been said, consists largely of rearranging what we know in order to find out what we do not know. Hence, to think creatively, we must be able to look afresh at what we normally take for granted.
George Kneller

It's easy to come up with new ideas; the hard part is letting go of what worked for you two years ago, but will soon be out of date.
Roger von Oech

The best way to have a good idea is to have a lot of ideas.
Dr. Linus Pauling

Discovery consists of seeing what everybody has seen and thinking what nobody has thought.
Albert von Szent-Gyorgy

To raise new questions, new possibilities, to regard old problems from a new angle, requires creative imagination and marks real advance in science.
Albert Einstein

There's a way to do it better—find it.
Thomas Edison

The essential part of creativity is not being afraid to fail.
Edwin H. Land

There is no doubt that creativity is the most important human resource of all. Without creativity, there would be no progress, and we would be forever repeating the same patterns.
Edward de Bono

Creativity is not the finding of a thing, but the making something out of it after it is found.
James Russell Lowell

The things we fear most in organizations—fluctuations, disturbances, imbalances—are the primary sources of creativity.
Margaret Wheatley

The achievement of excellence can only occur if the organization promotes a culture of creative dissatisfaction.
Lawrence Miller

Innovation— any new idea—by definition will not be accepted at first. It takes repeated attempts, endless demonstrations, monotonous rehearsals before innovation can be accepted and internalized by an organization. This requires courageous patience.
Warren Bennis

The uncreative mind can spot wrong answers, but it takes a very creative mind to spot wrong questions.
Anthony Jay

Creativity is thinking up new things. Innovation is doing new things.
Theodore Levitt

Innovation is the process of turning ideas into manufacturable and marketable form.
Watts Humprey

The innovation point is the pivotal moment when talented and motivated people seek the opportunity to act on their ideas and dreams.
W. Arthur Porter

Innovation distinguishes between a leader and a follower.
Steve Jobs

When you innovate, you've got to be prepared for everyone telling you you're nuts.
Larry Ellison

An enterprising person is one who comes across a pile of scrap metal and sees the making of a wonderful sculpture. An enterprising person is one who drives through an old decrepit part of town and sees a new housing development. An enterprising person is one who sees opportunity in all areas of life.
Jim Rohn

Innovation is the specific instrument of entrepreneurship—the act that endows resources with a new capacity to create wealth.
Peter Drucker

Never before in history has innovation offered promise of so much to so many in so short a time.
Bill Gates

Innovation is the central issue in economic prosperity.
Michael Porter

Once again, this nation has said there are no dreams too large, no innovation unimaginable and no frontiers beyond our reach.
John S. Herrington

The most successful people are those who are good at Plan B.
James Yorke

Just as energy is the basis of life itself and ideas the source of innovation, so is innovation the vital spark of all human change, improvement and progress.
Theodore Levitt

The best way to predict the future is to invent it.
Alan Kay

The world leaders in innovation and creativity will also be world leaders in everything else.
Harold R. McAlindon

Innovation is the creation of the new or the re-arranging of the old in a new way.
Michael Vance

To reach a goal you have never before attained, you must do things you have never before done.
Richard G. Scott

Change will happen because you make it happen.
Dr. Phil McGraw

Major improvements follow minor adjustments.
David DeFord

The course of our lives is seldom determined by great life-altering decisions. Our direction is often set by the small, day-to-day choices that chart the track on which we run. This is the substance of our lives—making choices.
Gordon B. Hinckley

Change before you have to.

Jack Welch

Chapter 4

Greatness

Only one man in a thousand is a leader of men -- the other 999 follow women.
Groucho Marx

You gain strength, courage and confidence by every experience in which you really stop to look fear in the face. You must do the thing you think you cannot do.
Eleanor Roosevelt

I am a leader by default, only because nature does not allow a vacuum.
Bishop Desmond Tutu

If one is lucky, a solitary fantasy can totally transform one million realities.
Maya Angelou

One can never consent to creep when one feels an impulse to soar.
Helen Keller

The quality of a leader is reflected in the standards they set for themselves.
Ray Kroc

Jingshen is the Mandarin word for spirit and vivacity. It is an important word for those who would lead, because above all things, spirit and vivacity set effective organizations apart from those that will decline and die.
James L. Hayes

The price of greatness is responsibility.
Winston Churchill

The task of leadership is not to put greatness into people, but to elicit it, for the greatness is there already.
John Buchan

Start doing the things you think should be done, and start being what you think society should become. Do you believe in free speech? Then speak freely. Do you love the truth? Then tell it. Do you believe in an open society? Then act in the open. Do you believe in a decent and humane society? Then behave decently and humanely.
Adam Michnik

If something comes to life in others because of you, then you have made an approach to immortality.
Norman Cousins

Effective leadership is the only competitive advantage that will endure. That's because leadership has two sides—what a person is (character) and what a person does (competence).
Stephen R. Covey

A great man shows his greatness by the way he treats little men.
Thomas Carlyle

Whoever renders service to many puts himself in line for greatness - great wealth, great return, great satisfaction, great reputation and great joy.
Jim Rohn

There is no greatness without a passion to be great, whether it's the aspiration of an athlete or an artist, a scientist, a parent, or a businessperson.
Anthony Robbins

It's not what you take but what you leave behind that defines greatness.
Edward Gardner

He is greatest whose strength carries up the most hearts by the attraction of his own.
Henry Ward Beecher

Nearly every man who develops an idea works at it up to the point where it looks impossible, and then gets discouraged. That's not the place to become discouraged.
Thomas Edison

It's kind of fun to do the impossible!
Walt Disney

The greatest use of life is to spend it for something that outlasts it.
William James

Strong lives are motivated by dynamic purposes; lesser ones exist on wishes and inclinations.
Kenneth Hildebrand

Chance can allow you to accomplish a goal every once in a while, but consistent achievement happens only if you love what you are doing.
Bart Conner

Do what you love and the money will follow.
Marsha Sinetar

The meaning of life is to give life meaning.
Ken Hudgins

We succeed only as we identify in life, or in war, or in anything else, a single overriding objective, and make all other considerations bend to that one objective.
Dwight D. Eisenhower

A difficult time can be more readily endured if we retain the conviction that our existence holds a purpose - a cause to pursue, a person to love, a goal to achieve.
John C. Maxwell

Outstanding people have one thing in common: an absolute sense of mission.
Zig Ziglar

Don't ask yourself what the world needs; ask yourself what makes you come alive. And then go and do that. Because what the world needs are people who have come alive.
Harold Whitman

When you discover your mission, you will feel its demand. It will fill you with enthusiasm and a burning desire to get to work on it.
W. Clement Stone

Find a purpose in life so big it will challenge every capacity to be at your best.
David O. MacKay

Service is the very purpose of life. It is the rent we pay for living on the planet.
Marian Wright Edelman

Good luck is another name for tenacity of purpose.
Ralph Waldo Emerson

Many persons have a wrong idea of what constitutes true happiness. It is not attained through self-gratification but through fidelity to a worthy purpose.
Helen Keller

Each one of us has a fire in our heart for something. It's our goal in life to find it and keep it lit.
Mary Lou Retton

Everyone has the power for greatness, not for fame but for greatness, because greatness is determined by service.
Martin Luther King, Jr.

There is more in us than we know. If we can be made to see it, perhaps, for the rest of our lives, we will be unwilling to settle for less.
Kurt Hahn

Somewhere, something incredible is waiting to be known.
Carl Sagan

Great men are true men, the men in whom nature has succeeded. They are not extraordinary - they are in the true order. It is the other species of men who are not what they ought to be.
Henri Frederic Amiel

Creativity means believing you have greatness.
Dr. Wayne W. Dyer

There are no great men, only great challenges that ordinary men are forced by circumstances to meet.
William F. Halsey

I shall not remain insignificant, I shall work in the world for mankind....I don't want to have lived in vain like most people. I want to be useful or bring enjoyment to all people, even those I've never met. I want to go on living, even after my death!
Anne Frank

A man, as a general rule, owes very little to what he is born with – a man is what he makes himself.
Alexander Graham Bell

Time and money spent in helping men do more for themselves is far better than mere giving.
Henry Ford

No great man ever complains of want of opportunity.
Ralph Waldo Emerson

Be not afraid of greatness; some are born great, some achieve greatness, and others have greatness thrust upon them.
William Shakespeare

No great man lives in vain. The history of the world is but the biography of great men.
Thomas Carlyle

Man is only truly great when he acts from his passions.
Benjamin Disraeli

Great men are like eagles, and build their nest on some lofty solitude.
Arthur Schopenhauer

I can't believe that God put us on this earth to be ordinary.
Lou Holtz

The ultimate is not to win, but to reach within the depths of your capabilities and to compete against yourself.
Billy Mills

It is the privilege of posterity to set matters right between those antagonists who, by their rivalry for greatness, divided a whole age.
Joseph Addison

Every great man is unique.
Ralph Waldo Emerson

Greatness after all, in spite of its name, appears to be not so much a certain size as a certain quality in human lives. It may be present in lives whose range is very small.
Phillips Brooks

Is it so bad, then, to be misunderstood? Pythagoras was misunderstood, and Socrates, and Jesus, and Luther, and Copernicus, and Galileo, and Newton, and every pure and wise spirit that ever took flesh. To be great is to be misunderstood.
Ralph Waldo Emerson

Do not confuse notoriety and fame with greatness. . . . For you see, greatness is a measure of one's spirit, not a result of one's rank in human affairs.
Sherman Finesilver

Let us consider the nature of true greatness in men. The people who can catch hold of men's minds and feelings and inspire them to do things bigger than themselves are the people who are remembered in history. . . . those who stir feelings and imagination and make men struggle toward perfection.
Henry Eyring

A great man will not trample upon a worm, nor sneak to an emperor.
Thomas Fuller

A desire for bigness has hurt many folks. Putting oneself in the limelight at the expense of others is a wrong idea of greatness. The secret of greatness rather than bigness is to acclimate oneself to one's place of service and be true to one's own convictions. A life of this kind of service will forever remain the measure of one's true greatness.
Richard W. Shelly, Jr.

Recipe for greatness - To bear up under loss, to fight the bitterness of defeat and the weakness of grief, to be victor over anger, to smile when tears are close, to resist evil men and base instincts, to hate hate and to love love, to go on when it would seem good to die, to seek ever after the glory and the dream, to look up with unquenchable faith in something evermore about to be, that is what any man can do, and so be great.
Zane Grey

. . . I want it said of me by those who knew me best, that I always plucked a thistle and planted a flower where I thought a flower would grow.

Abraham Lincoln

If any man seeks for greatness, let him forget greatness and ask for truth, and he will find both.

Horace Mann

Every great man is always being helped by everybody, for his gift is to get good out of all things and all persons.

John Ruskin

You are not here merely to make a living. You are here in order to enable the world to live more amply, with greater vision, with a finer spirit of hope and achievement. You are here to enrich the world, and you impoverish yourself if you forget the errand.

Woodrow Wilson

Some things have not changed since the dawn of history, and bid fair to last out time itself. One of these things is the capacity for greatness in man-his capacity for being often the master of the event -and sometimes even more-the changer of the course of history itself. This capacity for greatness is a very precious gift, and we are under a danger in our day of stifling it.

Dr. William Clyde de Vane

We make a living by what we get, but we make a life by what we give.

Winston Churchill

What lies behind us and what lies before us are small matters compared to what lies within us.
Ralph Waldo Emerson

Great minds discuss ideas, average minds discuss events, small minds discuss people.
Hyman Rickover

Everyone has a fair turn to be as great as he pleases.
Jeremy Collier

You are not here merely to make a living. You are here in order to enable the world to live more amply, with greater vision, with a finer spirit of hope and achievement. You are here to enrich the world, and you impoverish yourself if you forget the errand.
Woodrow Wilson

No man, who continues to add something to the material, intellectual and moral well-being of the place in which he lives, is left long without proper reward.
Booker T. Washington

Great minds have purposes, others have wishes.
Washington Irving

Chapter 5

The Leader as Servant

Good leaders must first become good servants.
Robert Greenleaf

You cannot be a leader, and ask other people to follow you, unless you know how to follow, too.
Sam Rayburn

The true leader serves.
Eugene B. Habecker

I don't know what your destiny will be, but one thing I know: The ones among you who will be really happy are those who have sought and found how to serve.
Albert Schweitzer

If you don't understand that you work for your mislabeled 'subordinates,' then you know nothing of leadership. You know only tyranny.
Dee Hock

Leadership is action, not position.
Donald H. McGannon

Leadership should be more participative than directive, more enabling than performing.
Mary D. Poole

The main characteristics of effective leadership are intelligence, integrity or loyalty, mystique, humor, discipline, courage, self sufficiency and confidence.
James L. Fisher

The first step to leadership is servanthood.
John C. Maxwell

Everything about business comes down to PEOPLE.
Bruce Cryer

Avoid having your ego so close to your position that when your position falls, your ego goes with it.
Colin Powell

You have to love people to serve them. Otherwise they will not allow you to serve them.
Hartman Rector

If leadership serves only the leader, it will fail. Ego satisfaction, financial gain, and status can all be valuable tools for a leader, but if they become the only motivations, they will eventually destroy a leader. Only when service for a common good is the primary purpose are you truly leading.
Sheila Murray Bethel

Servant-leadership is more than a concept, it is a fact. Any great leader, by which I also mean an ethical leader of any group, will see herself or himself as a servant of that group and will act accordingly.
M. Scott Peck

A person who is worthy of being a leader wants power not for himself, but in order to be of service.
Sam Ervin

There is no more noble occupation in the world than to assist another human being to help someone succeed.
Alan Loy McGinnis

You become a leader by helping others to the top. Helping your employees is as important, and many times more so, than trying to get the most work out of them.
William Cohen

Use power to help people. For we are given power neither to advance our own purposes nor to make a great show in the world, not a name. There is but one just use of power and it is to serve people.
George Bush

True leadership must be for the benefit of the followers, not to enrich the leader.
John C. Maxwell

None of us has gotten where we are solely by pulling ourselves up from our own bootstraps. We got here because somebody bent down and helped us.
Thurgood Marshall

It is one of the most beautiful compensations of this life that no man can sincerely try to help another without helping himself.
Ralph Waldo Emerson

You cannot teach a man anything; you can only help him find it within himself.
Galileo Galilei

In helping others, we shall help ourselves, for whatever good we give out completes the circle and comes back to us.
Flora Edwards

Successful people are always looking for opportunities to help others. Unsuccessful people are always asking, "What's in it for me?"
Brian Tracy

Help people become more motivated by guiding them to the source of their own power.
Paul G. Thomas

He that won't be counseled can't be helped.
Benjamin Franklin

I have found that being honest is the best technique I can use. Right up front, tell people what you're trying to accomplish and what you're willing to sacrifice to accomplish it.
Lee Iacocca

The best antidote I know for worry is work. The best medicine for despair is service. The best cure for weariness is the challenge of helping someone who is even more tired.
Gordon B. Hinckley

Chapter 6

Integrity

Integrity is the golden key which will unlock the door to almost any success
Howard W. Hunter

Leadership consists not in degrees of technique but in traits of character.
Lewis H. Lapham

Whoever is careless with the truth in small matters cannot be trusted with the important matters.
Albert Einstein

We must become the change we want to see.
Mahatma Gandhi

Nearly all men can stand adversity, but if you want to test a man's character, give him power.
Abraham Lincoln

I am a man of fixed and unbending principles, the first of which is to be flexible at all times.
Everett Dirksen

What is left when honor is lost?
Publilius Syrus

Personal integrity is as important as executive skill in business dealings.
Russell E. Palmer

A good conscience is a continual Christmas.
Benjamin Franklin

In looking for people to hire, you look for three qualities: integrity, intelligence, and energy. And if they don't have the first, the other two will kill you.
Warren Buffet

To be persuasive we must be believable; to be believable we must be credible; credible we must be truthful.
Edward R. Murrow

The chief lesson I have learned in a long life is that the only way you can make a man trustworthy is by trusting him; and the surest way to make him untrustworthy is to distrust him and show your distrust.
Henry L. Stimson

The man who trusts men will make fewer mistakes than he who distrusts them.
Camillo Benso di Cavour

There are seven things that will destroy us: Wealth without work; Pleasure without conscience; Knowledge without character; Religion without sacrifice; Politics without principle; Science without humanity; Business without ethics.
Mahatma Gandhi

Keep true, never be ashamed of doing right, decide on what you think is right and stick to it.
George Eliot

As a leader, you have to not only do the right thing, but be perceived to be doing the right thing. A consequence of seeking a leadership position is being put under intense public scrutiny, being held to high standards, and enhancing a reputation that is constantly under threat.
Jeffrey Sonnenfeld and Andrew Ward

Leadership is a combination of strategy and character. If you must be without one, be without the strategy.
H. Norman Schwarzkopf

Leaders who win the respect of others are the ones who deliver more than they promise, not the ones who promise more than they can deliver.
Mark Clement

People can be divided into two classes: those who go ahead and do something, and those people who sit still and inquire, why wasn't it done the other way?
Oliver Wendell Holmes

The supreme quality for leadership is unquestionably integrity. Without it, no real success is possible, no matter whether it is on a section gang, a football field, in an army, or in an office.
Dwight D. Eisenhower

There are many qualities that make a great leader. But having strong beliefs, being able to stick with them through popular and unpopular times, is the most important characteristic of a great leader.
Rudy Giuliani

A single lie destroys a whole reputation for integrity.
Baltasar Gracian

Example is not the main thing in influencing others, it is the only thing.
Albert Schweitzer

The ultimate measure of a man is not where he stands in moments of comfort, but where he stands at times of challenge and controversy.
Martin Luther King, Jr.

Character is much easier kept than recovered.
Thomas Paine

Your job gives you authority. Your behavior gives you respect.
Irwin Federman

Nothing is so potent as the silent influence of a good example.
James Kent

If leaders are careless about basic things - telling the truth, respecting moral codes, proper professional conduct - who can believe them on other issues?
James L. Hayes

No amount of ability is of the slightest avail without honor.
Andrew Carnegie

Honesty is the cornerstone of all success, without which confidence and ability to perform shall cease to exist.
Mary Kay Ash

Live so that when your children think of fairness and integrity, they think of you.
H. Jackson Brown, Jr.

Honor is better than honors.
Abraham Lincoln

Contrary to the cliche', genuinely nice guys most often finish first or very near it.
Malcolm S. Forbes

If you would lift me up you must be on higher ground.
Ralph Waldo Emerson

Always recognize that human individuals are ends, and do not use them as means to your end.
Immanuel Kant

Character is power.
Booker T. Washington

Complete and constant integrity is a great law of human conduct. There need to be some absolutes in life.
James E. Faust

If we live good lives, the times are also good. As we are, such are the times.
St. Augustine

You must never be fearful about what you are doing when it is right.
Rosa Parks

In matters of style, swim with the current; in matters of principle, stand like a rock.
Thomas Jefferson

People of character do the right thing, not because they think it will change the world but because they refuse to be changed by the world.
Michael Josephson

The height of your accomplishments will equal the depth of your convictions.
William F. Scolavino

True independence and freedom can only exist in doing what's right.
Brigham Young

I wish to be useful.
Nathan Hale

When we lower our sights to our daily tasks and lose sight of our overriding mission we suffer and so does the quality and passion of our work.
David DeFord

No true victory requires the sacrifice of our values.
David DeFord

I would rather be a man of conviction than a man of conformity.
Martin Luther King, Jr.

On some positions, Cowardice asks the question, "Is it safe?" Expediency asks the question, "Is it politic?" And Vanity comes along and asks the question, "Is it popular?" But Conscience asks the question, "Is it right?" And there comes a time when one must take a position that is neither safe, nor politic, nor popular, but he must do it because Conscience tells him it is right.
Martin Luther King, Jr.

As we express our gratitude, we must remember that the highest appreciation is not to utter words, but to live by them.
John Fitzgerald Kennedy

The best index to a person's character is (a) how he treats people who can't do him any good, and (b) how he treats people who can't fight back.
Abigail Van Buren

There is a very real relationship... between what you contribute and what you get out of this world.
Oscar Hammerstein II

If you are not generous with a meager income, you will never be generous with abundance.
Harold Nye

No man loses credit by being true to his principles.
George Q. Cannon

Confidence....thrives only on honesty, on honor, on the sacredness of obligations, on faithful protection and on unselfish performance. Without them, it cannot live.
Franklin D. Roosevelt

Honesty and transparency make you vulnerable. Be honest and transparent anyway.
Mother Teresa

When your heart speaks, take good notes.
Michael Angier

...my faith demands that I do whatever I can, wherever I am, whenever I can, for as long as I can with whatever I have to try to make a difference.
Jimmy Carter

We are not cisterns made for hoarding, we are channels made for sharing. God has given us two hands, one to receive with and the other to give with.
Billy Graham

You must never be fearful about what you are doing when it is right.
Rosa Parks

I've seen and met angels wearing the disguise of ordinary people living ordinary lives.
Tracy Chapman

My hope still is to leave the world a bit better than when I got here.
Jim Henson

Find some you really care about -- and live a life that shows it.
Kate Wolf

To do good things in the world, first you must know who you are and what gives meaning to your life.
Robert Browning

Great opportunities to help others seldom come, but small ones surround us every day.
Sally Koch

I have never been especially impressed by the heroics of people convinced that they are about to change the world, I am more awed by those who struggle to make one small difference after another.
Ellen Goodman

Great minds have purposes, others have wishes.
Washington Irving

A life is not important except in the impact it has on other lives.
Jackie Robinson

I think the purpose of life is to be useful, to be responsible, to be honorable, to be compassionate. It is, after all, to matter: to count, to stand for something, to have made some difference that you lived at all.
Leo C. Rosten

In every community, there is work to be done. In every nation, there are wounds to heal. In every heart, there is the power to do it.
Marianne Williamson

Believe in something larger than yourself... Get involved in the big ideas of your time.
Barbara Bush

Turn your life into a work of art, and let your soul show you where you need to go.
Cheryl Richardson

The purpose of life is a life of purpose.
Robert Byrne

We are not human beings on a spiritual journey; we are spiritual beings on a human journey.
Stephen R. Covey

Success is not so much what we have as it is what we are.
Jim Rohn

Success isn't something you chase. It's something you have to put forth the effort for constantly. Then maybe it'll come when you least expect it. Most people don't understand that.
Michael Jordan

The ability to discipline yourself to delay gratification in the short term in order to enjoy greater rewards in the long term is the indispensable prerequisite for success.
Brian Tracy

He who reigns within himself and rules his passions, desires, and fears is more than a king.
John Milton

Leadership is a potent combination of strategy and character. But if you must be without one, be without the strategy.
H. Norman Schwarzkopf

Nearly all men can stand adversity, but if you want to test a man's character give him power.
Abraham Lincoln

You can't build a reputation on what you're going to do.
Henry Ford

Chapter 7

A Leader Motivates

Kind words can be short and easy to speak, but their echoes are truly endless.
Mother Teresa

There's nothing more demoralizing than a leader who can't clearly articulate why we're doing what we're doing.
James Kouzes and Barry Posner

[Y]ou must unite your constituents around a common cause and connect with them as human beings.
James Kouzes and Barry Posner

Most important, leaders can conceive and articulate goals that lift people out of their petty preoccupations and unite them in pursuit of objectives worthy of their best efforts.
John Gardner

If your actions inspire others to dream more, learn more, do more and become more, you are a leader.
John Quincy Adams

The key to successful leadership today is influence, not authority.
> **Kenneth Blanchard**

Keep your fears to yourself, but share your inspiration with others.
> **Robert Louis Stevenson**

Our chief want is someone who will inspire us to be what we know we could be.
> **Ralph Waldo Emerson**

A leader's role is to raise people's aspirations for what they can become and to release their energies so they will try to get there.
> **David R. Gergen**

I am personally convinced that one person can be a change catalyst, a "transformer" in any situation, any organization. Such an individual is yeast that can leaven an entire loaf. It requires vision, initiative, patience, respect, persistence, courage, and faith to be a transforming leader.
> **Stephen R. Covey**

A big man is one who makes us feel bigger when we are with him.
> **John C. Maxwell**

The first task of a leader is to keep hope alive.
> **Joe Batten**

It is the nature of man to rise to greatness if greatness is expected of him.
John Steinbeck

The great difference between the real leader and the pretender is that the one sees into the future, while the other regards only the present; the one lives by the day, and acts upon expediency; the other acts on enduring principles and for the immortality.
Edmund Burke

Leadership is the ability of a single individual through his or her actions to motivate others to higher levels of achievement.
Buck Rodgers

Leadership is a matter of having people look at you and gain confidence, seeing how you react. If you're in control, they're in control.
Tom Landry

Somewhere, sometime, the leader within each of us may get the call to step forward.
James M. Kouzes and Barry Z. Posner

The job of leaders is to think from their heads, communicate from their hearts and to act from their guts.
David Gaster

Lead and inspire people. Don't try to manage and manipulate people. Inventories can be managed but people must be lead.
Ross Perot

The goal of many leaders is to get people to think more highly of the leader. The goal of a great leader is to help people to think more highly of themselves.
J. Carla Nortcutt

Leaders we admire do not place themselves at the center; they place others there.
James Kouzes and Barry Posner

Leadership flows from the minds of followers more than from the titles of leaders, more from the perception of willing followers than from anointment.
Lane Secretan

The motivating team leader is that one person with a dream for the future.
Dr. Lewis Losoncy

I've learned that people will forget what you said, people will forget what you did, but people will never forget how you made them feel.
Maya Angelou

A master can tell you what he expects of you. A teacher, though, awakens your own expectations.
Patricia Neal

High achievement always takes place in the framework of high expectation.
Jack Kinder

By asking for the impossible we obtain the best possible.
Giovanni Niccolini

Before you can inspire with emotion, you must be swamped with it yourself. Before you can move their tears, your own must flow. To convince them, you must yourself believe.
Winston Churchill

Chapter 8

Build Future Leaders

Don't tell people how to do things, tell them what to do and let them surprise you with their results.
George S. Patton

Leadership is the art of getting someone else to do something you want done because he wants to do it.
Dwight D. Eisenhower

A leader is a dealer in hope.
Napoleon Bonaparte

Delegating work works, provided the one delegating works, too.
Robert Half

The best executive is the one who has sense enough to pick good men to do what he wants done, and self-restraint to keep from meddling with them while they do it.
Theodore Roosevelt

I start with the premise that the function of leadership is to produce more leaders, not more followers.
Ralph Nader

The final test of a leader is that he leaves behind him in other men the conviction and the will to carry on. . . . The genius of a good leader is to leave behind him a situation which common sense, without the grace of genius, can deal with successfully.
Walter Lippmann

When the best leader's work is done the people say, "We did it ourselves!"
Lao-tsu

The final test of a leader is that he leaves behind him in other men the conviction and will to carry on.
Walter J. Lippmann

Leadership should be born out of the understanding of the needs of those who would be affected by it.
Marian Anderson

No man will make a great leader who wants to do it all himself, or to get all the credit for doing it.
Andrew Carnegie

Probably my best quality as a coach is that I ask a lot of challenging questions and let the person come up with the answer.
Phil Dixon

Never hire or promote in your own image.
Dee W. Hock

A community is like a ship; everyone ought to be prepared to take the helm.
Henrik Ibsen

The manager asks how and when; the leader asks what and why.
Warren Bennis

How do you know you have won? When the energy is coming the other way and when your people are visibly growing individually and as a group.
Sir John Harvey-Jones

As a leader, you're probably not doing a good job unless your employees can do a good impression of you when you're not around.
Patrick Lencioni

Look over your shoulder now and then to be sure someone's following you.
Henry Gilmer

Leadership is not magnetic personality that can just as well be a glib tongue. It is not "making friends and influencing people", that is flattery. Leadership is lifting a person's vision to higher sights, the raising of a person's performance to a higher standard, the building of a personality beyond its normal limitations.
Peter Drucker

Catch someone doing something right.
Kenneth Blanchard and Spencer Johnson

If you pick the right people and give them the opportunity to spread their wings—and put compensation as a carrier behind it—you almost don't have to manage them.
Jack Welch

Surround yourself with the best people you can find, delegate authority, and don't interfere as long as the policy you've decided upon is being carried out.
Ronald Reagan

Always recognize that human individuals are ends, and do not use them as means to your end.
Immanuel Kant

Don't equate activity with efficiency. You are paying your key people to see the big picture. Don't let them get bogged down in a lot of meaningless meetings and paper shuffling.
Harvey Mackay

Hire people who are better than you are, then leave them to get on with it . . . ; Look for people who will aim for the remarkable, who will not settle for the routine.
David Ogilvy

When hiring key employees, there are only two qualities to look for: judgment and taste. Almost everything else can be bought by the yard.
John W. Gardner

A desk is a dangerous place from which to view the world.
                                              John Le Carré

I believe the real difference between success and failure in a corporation can be very often traced to the question of how well the organization brings out the great energies and talents of its people.
                                              Thomas J. Watson, Jr.

Focus on a few key objectives ... I only have three things to do. I have to choose the right people, allocate the right number of dollars, and transmit ideas from one division to another with the speed of light. So I'm really in the business of being the gatekeeper and the transmitter of ideas.
                                              Jack Welch

So much of what we call management consists in making it difficult for people to work.
                                              Peter Drucker

Leadership is a serving relationship that has the effect of facilitating human development.
                                              Ted Ward

The conventional definition of management is getting work done through people, but real management is developing people through work.
                                              Agha Hasan Abedi

The best leaders are those most interested in surrounding themselves with assistants and associates smarter than they are. They are frank in admitting this and are willing to pay for such talents.

Amos Parrish

People are definitely a company's greatest asset. It doesn't make any difference whether the product is cars or cosmetics. A company is only as good as the people it keeps.

Mary Kay Ash

It takes leaders to grow other leaders.

Ray Blunt

Coaching isn't an addition to a leader's job; it's an integral part of it.

George S. Odiorne

It is literally true that you can succeed best and quickest by helping others to succeed.

Napoleon Hill

As we look ahead into the next century, leaders will be those who empower others.

Bill Gates

It is only as we develop others that we permanently succeed.

Harvey S. Firestone

One measure of leadership is the caliber of people who choose to follow you.
                                          Dennis A. Peer

Chapter 9

Respect for Associates

Trust men and they will be true to you; treat them greatly, and they will show themselves great.
Ralph Waldo Emerson

Treat people as if they were what they should be, and you help them become what they are capable of becoming.
Johann Wolfgang von Goethe

The boss drives people; the leader coaches them. The boss depends on authority; the leader on good will. The boss inspires fear; the leader inspires enthusiasm. The boss says I ; The leader says WE . The boss fixes the blame for the breakdown; the leader fixes the breakdown. The boss says, GO; the leader says LET'S GO!
H. Gordon Selfridge

Respect the man, and he will do the more.
James Howell

Never tell people how to do things. Tell them what to do and they will surprise you with their ingenuity.
George S. Patton

People ask the difference between a leader and a boss. The leader works in the open, and the boss in covert. The leader leads, and the boss drives.
Theodore Roosevelt

A good manager is a man who isn't worried about his own career but rather the careers of those who work for him.
Henry S. M. Burns

The greatest administrators do not achieve production through constraints and limitations. They provide opportunities.
Lao-Tze

A leader is best when people barely know he exists, when his work is done, his aim fulfilled, they will say: We did it ourselves.
Lao-Tze

A leader takes people where they want to go. A great leader takes people where they don't necessarily want to go, but ought to be.
Rosalynn Carter

Do not follow where the path may lead. Go instead where there is no path and leave a trail.
Muriel Strode

Leadership is getting someone to do what they don't want to do, to achieve what they want to achieve.
Tom Landry

The challenge of leadership is to be strong, but not rude; be kind, but not weak; be bold, but not bully; be thoughtful, but not lazy; be humble, but not timid; be proud, but not arrogant; have humor, but without folly.
Jim Rohn

You manage things; you lead people.
Grace Murray Hopper

The best executive is the one who has sense enough to pick good men to do what he wants done, and self-restraint enough to keep from meddling with them while they do it.
Theodore Roosevelt

Outstanding leaders go out of their way to boost the self-esteem of their personnel. If people believe in themselves, it's amazing what they can accomplish.
Sam Walton

No man will make a great leader who wants to do it all himself, or to get all the credit for doing it.
Andrew Carnegie

I have three precious things which I hold fast and prize. The first is gentleness; the second is frugality; the third is humility, which keeps me from putting myself before others. Be gentle and you can be bold; be frugal and you can be liberal; avoid putting yourself before others and you can become a leader among men.
Lao-Tze

He who has never learned to obey cannot be a good commander.
Aristotle

The key to successful leadership today is influence, not authority.
Ken Blanchard

The first responsibility of a leader is to define reality. The last is to say thank you. In between, the leader is a servant.
Max DuPree

You do not lead by hitting people over the head - that's assault, not leadership.
Dwight D. Eisenhower

Respect a man, he will do the more.
James Howell

Lift, Lead and Love.
Spencer W. Kimball

Rule a kingdom as though you were cooking a small fish -don't overdo it.
Lao-Tze

To command is to serve, nothing more and nothing less.
Andre Malraux

Leadership is an action, not a position.
Donald H. McGannon

Winners get to the top and turn around to see those they have defeated. Leaders get to the top and turn around to help others achieve the same.
Dan Churches

The office of government is not to confer happiness, but to give men the opportunity to work out happiness for themselves.
William Channing

You and I can never do a kindness too soon, for we never know how soon it will be too late.
Ralph Waldo Emerson

In organizations, real power and energy is generated through relationships. The patterns of relationships and the capacities to form them are more important than tasks, functions, roles, and positions.
Margaret Wheatley

Catch someone doing something right.
Kenneth Blanchard and Spencer Johnson

Leaders don't force people to follow—they invite them on a journey.
Charles S. Lauer

Leadership is practiced not so much in words as in attitude and in actions.
Harold Geneen

Chapter 10

Communication Must Travel Both Ways

The ear of the leader must ring with the voices of the people.
            Woodrow Wilson

Silence is a source of great strength.
            Lao Tzu

The most basic of all human needs is the need to understand and be understood. The best way to understand people is to listen to them.
            Ralph Nichols

Bore, n.: A person who talks when you wish him to listen.
            Ambrose Bierce

It's a rare person who wants to hear what he doesn't want to hear.
            Dick Cavett

Just because I didn't do what you told me, doesn't mean I wasn't listening to you!
            Hank Ketcham

There is no such thing as a worthless conversation, provided you know what to listen for. And questions are the breath of life for a conversation.
James Nathan Miller

You cannot truly listen to anyone and do anything else at the same time.
M. Scott Peck

There's a big difference between showing interest and really taking interest.
Michael P. Nichols

Man's inability to communicate is a result of his failure to listen effectively.
Carl Rogers

Big egos have little ears.
Robert Schuller

A good listener is not only popular everywhere, but after a while he gets to know something.
Wilson Mizner

Listening, not imitation, may be the sincerest form of flattery.
Dr Joyce Brothers

Wisdom is the reward for a lifetime of listening ... when you'd have preferred to talk.
D. J. Kaufman

There are people who, instead of listening to what is being said to them, are already listening to what they are going to say themselves.
Albert Guinon

No man ever listened himself out of a job.
Calvin Coolidge

Be a good listener. Your ears will never get you in trouble.
Frank Tyger

I only wish I could find an institute that teaches people how to listen. Business people need to listen at least as much as they need to talk. Too many people fail to realize that real communication goes in both directions.
Lee Iacocca

Seek first to understand, then to be understood.
Stephen R. Covey

To say that a person feels listened to means a lot more than just their ideas get heard. It's a sign of respect. It makes people feel valued.
Deborah Tannen

The best salespeople are great listeners—that's how you find out what the buyer wants.
Larry Wilson and Spencer Johnson

Without credible communication, and a lot of it, the hearts and minds of others are never captured.
John P. Kotter

Just being available and attentive is a great way to use listening as a management tool. Some employees will come in, talk for twenty minutes, and leave having solved their problems entirely by themselves.
Nicholas V. Luppa

I would say that listening to the other person's emotions may be the most important thing I've learned in twenty years of business.
Heath Herber

Of all the skills of leadership, listening is the most valuable—and one of the least understood. Most captains of industry listen only sometimes, and they remain ordinary leaders. But a few, the great ones, never stop listening. That's how they get word before anyone else of unseen problems and opportunities.
Peter Nulty

A good listener tries to understand what the other person is saying. In the end he may disagree sharply, but because he disagrees, he wants to know exactly what it is he is disagreeing with.
Kenneth A. Wells

We listened to what our customers wanted and acted on what they said. Good things happen when you pay attention.
John F. Smith

You learn when you listen. You earn when you listen— not just money, but respect.
Harvey Mackay

I remind myself every morning: Nothing I say this day will teach me anything. So if I'm going to learn, I must do it by listening.
Larry King

To learn through listening, practice it naively and actively. Naively means that you listen openly, ready to learn something, as opposed to listening defensively, ready to rebut. Listening actively means you acknowledge what you heard and act accordingly.
Betsy Sanders

The key to success is to get out into the store and listen to what the associates have to say. It's terribly important for everyone to get involved. Our best ideas come from clerks and stockboys.
Sam Walton

The most important single ingredient in the formula of success is knowing how to get along with people.
Theodore Roosevelt

The fields of industry are strewn with the bones of those organizations whose leadership became infested with dryrot, who believed in taking instead of giving . . . who didn't realize that the only assets that could not be replaced easily were the human ones.
Le Roy H. Kurtz

Accept the fact that we have to treat almost anybody as a volunteer.
Peter Drucker

The best executive is one who has sense enough to pick good people to do what he wants done, and self-restraint enough to keep from meddling with them while they do it.
Theodore Roosevelt

Much of leadership is about finding balance between two often-conflicting activities: asserting authority and responding to others' needs.
Belle Linda Halpern and Kathy Lubar

Be not angry that you cannot make others as you wish them to be, since you cannot make yourself as you wish to be.
Thomas a Kempis

Trust men and they will be true to you: treat them greatly and they will show themselves great.
Ralph Waldo Emerson

Nothing grows well without space and air.
Patricia Monaghan

The great paradox of the 21st century is that, in this age of powerful technology, the biggest problems we face internationally are problems of the human soul.
Ralph Peters

When dealing with people, remember you are not dealing with creatures of logic, but creatures of emotion.
Dale Carnegie

I am convinced that nothing we do is more important than hiring and developing people. At the end of the day you bet on people, not on strategies.
Larry Bossidy

Kind words can be short and easy to speak, but their echoes are truly endless.
Mother Teresa

Truly great leaders spend as much time collecting and acting upon feedback as they do providing it.
Alexander Lucia

The best way to persuade people is with your ears - by listening to them.
Dean Rusk

Chapter 11

Courage to Seize Opportunities

Don't be afraid to take a big step when one is indicated. You can't cross a chasm in two small steps.
David Lloyd George

The future is taking shape now in our own beliefs and in the courage of our leaders. Ideas and leadership -- not natural or social 'forces' -- are the prime movers in human affairs.
George Roche

Not everything that is faced can be changed. But nothing can be changed until it is faced.
James Baldwin

The world is round and the place which may seem like the end, may also be only the beginning.
Ivy Baker Priest

I cannot give you the formula for success, but I can give you the formula for failure: which is: Try to please everybody.
Herbert B. Swope

A leader must have the courage to act against an expert's advice.
James Callaghan

It's the same each time with progress. First they ignore you, then they say you're mad, then dangerous, then there's a pause and then you can't find anyone who disagrees with you.
Tony Benn

Creativity can solve almost any problem. The creative act, the defeat of habit by originality, overcomes everything. George Lois
If you're not prepared to be wrong, you'll never come up with anything original.
Sir Ken Robinson

Courage is rightly esteemed the first of human qualities ... because it is the quality which guarantees all others.
Winston Churchill

You gain strength, courage, and confidence by every experience in which you really stop to look fear in the face.
Eleanor Roosevelt

The desire for safety stands against every great and noble enterprise.
Tacitus

I love the man that can smile in trouble that can gather strength from distress, and grow brave by reflections.
Thomas Paine

Courage is doing what you're afraid to do. There can be no courage unless you're scared.
Eddie Rickenbacker

One man with courage makes a majority.
Andrew Jackson

What separates the winners from the losers is how a person reacts to each new twist of fate.
Donald Trump

Courage is not limited to the battlefield or the Indianapolis 500 or bravely catching a thief in your house. The real tests of courage are much quieter. They are the inner tests, like remaining faithful when nobody's looking, like enduring pain when the room is empty, like standing alone when you're misunderstood.
Charles Swindoll

Courage is being scared to death—but saddling up anyway.
John Wayne

In the age-old contest between popularity and principle, only those willing to lose for their convictions are deserving of posterity's approval.
Gerald R. Ford

Success on any major scale requires you to accept responsibility. . . . In the final analysis, the one quality that all successful people have is the ability to take on responsibility.
Michael Korda

The man who complains about the way the ball bounces is likely to be the one who dropped it.
Lou Holtz

Being responsible sometimes means pissing people off.
Colin Powell

You must take personal responsibility. You cannot change the circumstances, the seasons, or the wind, but you can change yourself.
Jim Rohn

The reason people blame things on the previous generation is that there's only one other choice.
Doug Larson

Ninety-nine percent of all failures come from people who have a habit of making excuses.
George Washington Carver

All blame is a waste of time. No matter how much fault you find with another, and regardless of how much you blame him, it will not change you.
Wayne Dyer

Success is going from failure to failure without a loss of enthusiasm.
Winston Churchill

The greatest test of courage on the earth is to bear defeat without losing heart.
R. G. Ingersoll

A timid person is frightened before a danger, a coward during the time, and a courageous person afterwards.
Paul Richter

Courage is the art of being the only one who knows you're scared to death!
Earl Wilson

It is curious—curious that physical courage should be so common in the world, and moral courage so rare.
Mark Twain

The greatest mistake we make is living in constant fear that we will make one.
John C. Maxwell

A ship is safe in harbor, but that's not what ships are for.
William Shedd

Courage doesn't always roar. Sometimes courage is the quiet voice at the end of the day saying, "I will try again tomorrow.
Mary Anne Radmacher

Courage is the power to let go of the familiar.
Raymond Lindquist

Courage is simply the willingness to be afraid and act anyway.
Dr. Robert Anthony

You will never do anything in this world without courage. It is the greatest quality of the mind next to honor.
Aristotle

There is nothing wrong with change, if it is in the right direction.
Winston Churchill

Action conquers fear.
Peter Nivio Zarlenga

To map out a course of action and follow it to an end requires courage.
Ralph Waldo Emerson

When you cannot make up your mind which of two evenly balanced courses of action you should take - choose the bolder.
William Joseph Slim

Whenever you see a successful business, someone once made a courageous decision.
Peter Drucker

Successful leaders have the courage to take action while others hesitate.
John C. Maxwell

Often the difference between a successful person and a failure is not one has better abilities or ideas, but the courage that one has to bet on one's ideas, to take a calculated risk - and to act.
Maxwell Maltz

Impossible situations can become possible miracles.
Robert H. Schuller

Out of difficulties grow miracles.
Jean De La Bruyere

It is not the mountain we conquer, but ourselves
Sir Edmund Hillary

Great things are done when men and mountains meet.
William Blake

Press on. Obstacles are seldom the same size tomorrow as they are today.
Robert H. Schuller

Most of our obstacles would melt away if, instead of cowering before them, we should make up our minds to walk boldly through them.
Orison Swett Marden

If you find a path with no obstacles, it probably doesn't lead anywhere.
Frank A. Clark

It still holds true that man is most uniquely human when he turns obstacles into opportunities.
Eric Hoffer

Obstacles will look large or small to you according to whether you are large or small.
Orison Swett Marden

History has demonstrated that the most notable winners usually encountered heartbreaking obstacles before they triumphed. They won because they refused to become discouraged by their defeats.
B. C. Forbes

Stand up to your obstacles and do something about them. You will find that they haven't half the strength you think they have.
Norman Vincent Peale

It's the constant and determined effort that breaks down all resistance, sweeps away all obstacles.
Claude M. Bristol

Patience and perseverance have a magical effect before which difficulties disappear and obstacles vanish.
John Quincy Adams

If a window of opportunity appears, don't pull down the shade.
Tom Peters

Opportunity is often difficult to recognize; we usually expect it to beckon us with beepers and billboards.
William Arthur Ward

Jumping at several small opportunities may get us there more quickly than waiting for one big one to come along.
Hugh Allen

Men who are resolved to find a way for themselves will always find opportunities enough; and if they do not find them, they will make them.
Samuel Smiles

Nothing is more expensive than a missed opportunity.
H. Jackson Brown Jr.

Wherever there is danger, there lurks opportunity; whenever there is opportunity, there lurks danger. The two are inseparable. They go together.
Earl Nightingale

Opportunity rarely knocks on your door. Knock rather on opportunity's door if you ardently wish to enter.
B. C. Forbes

Start where you are. Distant fields always look greener, but opportunity lies right where you are.
Robert Collier

A window of opportunity won't open itself.
Dave Weinbaum

Opportunities multiply as they are seized.
Sun Tzu

Great lives are the culmination of great thoughts followed by great actions.
Peter Sinclair

Trouble is only opportunity in work clothes.
Henry J. Kaiser

Opportunities are usually disguised as hard work, so most people don't recognize them.
Ann Landers

A pessimist sees the difficulty in every opportunity; an optimist sees the opportunity in every difficulty.
Winston Churchill

Take off the blinders. You have to see opportunity before you can seize it.
Greg Hickman

Become a possibilitarian. No matter how dark things seem to be or actually are, raise your sights and see possibilities—always see them for they're always there.
Norman Vincent Peale

I do not think that there is any other quality so essential to success of any kind as the quality of perseverance. It overcomes almost everything, even nature.
John D. Rockefeller

Your biggest break can come from never quitting. Being at the right place at the right time can only happen when you keep moving toward the next opportunity.
Arthur Pine

The antidote to worry is purposeful action.
Brian Tracy

All growth is a leap in the dark, a spontaneous, unpremeditated act without benefit of experience.
Henry Miller

Security is mostly a superstition. It does not exist in nature, nor do the children of men as a whole experience it. Avoiding danger is no safer in the long run than outright exposure. Life is a daring adventure or nothing at all.
Helen Keller

The most rewarding things you do in life are often the ones that look like they cannot be done.
Arnold Palmer

Idealists, foolish enough to throw caution to the winds, have advanced mankind and have enriched the world.
Emma Goldman

It is our attitude at the beginning of a difficult task which, more than anything else, will affect its successful outcome.
William James

When you choose your behavior and your thoughts, you choose the consequences.
Dr. Phil McGraw

Often our attitudes bring about the treatment life hands us. Through our attitudes we can influence whether we become conquerors or victims.
David DeFord

The biggest lesson I have ever learned is the stupendous importance of what we think. If I knew what you think, I would know what you are, for your thoughts make you what you are; by changing our thoughts, we can change our lives.
Dale Carnegie

You are the possessor of a great and wonderful power. This power, when properly applied, will bring confidence instead of timidity, calmness instead of confusion, poise instead of restlessness, and peace of mind in place of heartache. What is your greatest power? The power to choose.
J. Martin Kohe

There are no great people in this world, only great challenges which ordinary people rise to meet.
William Frederick Halsey, Jr.

The difference between whether you say, 'I wish I would have,' or 'I'm glad I did,' at the end of your life is whether or not you take decisive action during your life.
Chris Widener

We are continually faced with great opportunities brilliantly disguised as unsolvable problems.
Lee Iacocca

The faster the pitch the farther the ball will fly when we solidly connect. The more difficult the challenge, the greater the reward for meeting it squarely.
David DeFord

Courage means to keep working a relationship, to continue seeking solutions to difficult problems, and to stay focused during stressful periods.
Denis Waitley

Strength does not come from winning. Your struggles develop your strengths. When you go through hardships and decide not to surrender, that is strength.
Arnold Schwarzenegger

When we meet real tragedy in life, we can react in two ways—either by losing hope and falling into self-destructive habits or by using the challenge to find our inner strength.
The Dalai Lama

Comfort and prosperity have never enriched the world as much as adversity.
Billy Graham

Sometimes you win and sometimes you learn.
Robert Kiyosaki

The optimist, as you probably know, is a person who, when he wears out his shoes, just figures he's back on his feet.
Hartman Rector, Jr.

The value of a thing lies in the cost of attaining it.
David DeFord

Growth means change, and change involves risk, stepping from the known to the unknown.
George Shinn

Reach out and open the door that no one thought could be opened. Life is behind it.
Kelly Ann Rothaus

If you risk nothing, then you risk everything.
Geena Davis

Courage is contagious. When a brave man takes a stand, the spines of others are often stiffened.
Billy Graham

Never let your head hang down. Never give up and sit down and grieve. Find another way. And don't pray when it rains if you don't pray when the sun shines.
Leroy "Satchel" Paige

A setback will never defeat you. Only yielding to the setback can do that.
David DeFord

I am never down. I am either up or getting up!"
John C. Maxwell

Difficult times have helped me to understand better than before how infinitely rich and beautiful life is in every way and that so many things that one goes worrying about are of no importance whatsoever.
Isak Dinesen

Behind every success is a succession of failures.
Rick Beneteau

The person interested in success has to learn to view failure as a healthy, inevitable part of the process of getting to the top.
Dr. Joyce Brothers

The successful man will profit from his mistakes and try again in a different way.
Dale Carnegie

Even a mistake may turn out to be the one thing necessary to a worthwhile achievement.
Henry Ford

The trouble in America is not that we are making too many mistakes, but that we are making too few.
Philip Knight

The man who makes no mistakes does not usually make anything.
Theodore Roosevelt

A life spent making mistakes is not only more honorable, but more useful than a life spent doing nothing.
George Bernard Shaw

Prosperity discovers vice, adversity discovers virtue.
Francis Bacon

It's not that I'm so smart, it's just that I stay with problems longer.
Albert Einstein

To swear off making mistakes is very easy. All you have to do is swear off having ideas.
Leo Burnett

Victory is sweetest when you've known defeat.
Malcolm Forbes

You may have to fight a battle more than once to win it.
Margaret Thatcher

Failure is a detour, not a dead-end street.
Zig Ziglar

I've missed more than 9,000 shots in my career. I have lost almost 300 games. On 26 occasions I've been entrusted to take the game winning shot…and missed. And I have failed over and over and over again in my life. And that's why…I succeed.
Michael Jordan

There are many qualities that make a great leader. But having strong beliefs, being able to stick with them through popular and unpopular times is the most important characteristic of a great leader.
Rudy Giuliani

The people cannot look up to a leader who has his ear to the ground.
Winston Churchill

Why not go out on a limb? Isn't that where the fruit is?
Frank Scully

Progress always involves risk; you can't steal second base and keep your foot on first.
Frederick Wilcox

Whenever you see a successful business, someone once made a courageous decision.
Peter Drucker

When you cannot make up your mind which of two evenly balanced courses of action you should take—choose the bolder.
W. J. Slim

Great crises produce great men and great deeds of courage.
John F. Kennedy

In the middle of difficulty lies opportunity.
Albert Einstein

Each problem has hidden in an opportunity so powerful that it literally dwarfs the problem. The greatest success stories were created by people who recognized a problem a turned it into an opportunity.
Joseph Sugarman

A wise man will make more opportunities than he finds.
Francis Bacon

Opportunity...often it comes in the form of misfortune, or temporary defeat.
Napoleon Hill

Opportunities? They are all around us...there is power lying latent everywhere waiting for the observant eye to discover it.
Orison Swett Marden

Opportunity dances with those who are ready on the dance floor.
H. Jackson Brown Jr.

Too many people are thinking of security instead of opportunity. They seem more afraid of life than death.
James F. Byrnes

Opportunity does not knock, it presents itself when you beat down the door.
Kyle Chandler

Trouble is only opportunity in work clothes.
Henry J. Kaiser

When written in Chinese, the word 'crisis' is composed of two characters. One represents danger and the other represents opportunity.
John F. Kennedy

It is often hard to distinguish between the hard knocks in life and those of opportunity.
Frederick Philipse

The more you seek security, the less of it you have. But the more you seek opportunity, the more likely it is that you will achieve the security that you desire.
Brian Tracy

My motto was always to keep swinging. Whether I was in a slump or feeling badly or having trouble off the field, the only thing to do was keep swinging.
Hank Aaron

The important thing is to dare to dream big, and then take action to make it come true.
Joe Girard

You may have a fresh start any moment you choose, for this thing that we call 'failure' is not the falling down, but the staying down.
Mary Pickford

The trouble is, if you don't risk anything, you risk even more.
Erica Jong

Uncertainty will always be part of the taking charge process.
                                Harold Geneen

All serious daring starts from within.
                                Eudora Welty

In matters of style, swim with the current; in matters of principle, stand like a rock.
                                Thomas Jefferson

When nothing is sure, everything is possible.
                                Margaret Drabble

Cautious, careful people, always casting about to preserve their reputation and social standing, never can bring about a reform.
                                Susan B. Anthony

Do you want to be safe and good, or do you want to take a chance and be great?
                                Jimmy Johnson

It is much safer to obey than to rule.
                                Thomas A. Kempis

Never forget that only dead fish swim with the stream.
                                Malcolm Muggeridge

You don't concentrate on risks. You concentrate on results. No risk is too great to prevent the necessary job from getting done.
                                Chuck Yeager

Far better it is to dare mighty things, to win glorious triumphs, even though checkered by failure, than to take rank with those poor spirits who neither enjoy much nor suffer much, because they live in the grey twilight that knows not victory nor defeat.
Theodore Roosevelt

Chapter 12

Teamwork

The leader is one who mobilizes others toward a goal shared by leaders and followers. ... Leaders, followers and goals make up the three equally necessary supports for leadership.
Gary Wills

My own definition of leadership is this: The capacity and the will to rally men and women to a common purpose and the character that inspires confidence.
General Montgomery

High sentiments always win in the end, The leaders who offer blood, toil, tears and sweat always get more out of their followers than those who offer safety and a good time. When it comes to the pinch, human beings are heroic.
George Orwell

The important thing to recognize is that it takes a team, and the team ought to get credit for the wins and the losses. Successes have many fathers, failures have none.
Philip Caldwell

Define your business goals clearly so that others can see them as you do.
George F. Burns

You can buy a person's hands but you can't buy his heart. His heart is where his enthusiasm, his loyalty is.
Stephen R. Covey

An empowered organization is one in which individuals have the knowledge, skill, desire, and opportunity to personally succeed in a way that leads to collective organizational success.
Stephen R. Covey

Teamwork is the ability to work together toward a common vision. The ability to direct individual accomplishments toward organizational objectives. It is the fuel that allows common people to attain uncommon results.
Andrew Carnegie

None of us is as smart as all of us.
Ken Blanchard

People who work together will win, whether it be against complex football defenses, or the problems of modern society."
Vince Lombardi

Coming together is a beginning. Keeping together is progress. Working together is success.
Henry Ford

The ratio of We's to I's is the best indicator of the development of a team.
Lewis B. Ergen

Synergy is the highest activity of life; it creates new untapped alternatives; it values and exploits the mental, emotional, and psychological differences between people.
Stephen R. Covey

The key elements in the art of working together are how to deal with change, how to deal with conflict, and how to reach our potential...the needs of the team are best met when we meet the needs of individuals persons.
Max DePree

Talent wins games, but teamwork and intelligence wins championships.
Michael Jordan

When a team outgrows individual performance and learns team confidence, excellence becomes a reality.
Joe Paterno

No one can whistle a symphony. It takes an orchestra to play it.
H. E. Luccock

Effective teamwork is all about making a good, well-balanced salad not whipping individuals into a single batch of V8.
Sandra Richardson

All winning teams are goal-oriented. Teams like these win consistently because everyone connected with them concentrates on specific objectives. They go about their business with blinders on; nothing will distract them from achieving their aims.
Lou Holtz

In order to have a winner, the team must have a feeling of unity; every player must put the team first-ahead of personal glory.
Paul "Bear" Bryant

Individual commitment to a group effort — that is what makes a team work a company work, a society work, a civilization work.
Vince Lombardi

Seek first to understand, then to be understood.
Stephen R. Covey

A good leader takes a little more than his share of the blame, a little less than his share of the credit.
Abraham H. Glasgow

My grandfather once told me that there were two kinds of people: those who do the work and those who take the credit. He told me to try to be in the first group. There is much less competition.
Indira Gandhi

Until all of us have made it, none of us have made it.
Rosemary Brown

Vision comes alive when everyone sees where his or her contribution makes a difference.
Ken Blanchard

Good leadership is motivating and mobilizing others to accomplish a task or to think in ways that are for the benefit of all concerned.
Don Page

Few, if any, forces in human affairs are as powerful as shared vision.
Peter Senge

If we want people's intelligence and support, we must welcome them as co-creators. People only support what they create.
Margaret J. Wheatley

It is amazing what you can accomplish if you do not care who gets the credit.
Harry S Truman

I not only use all the brains I have, but all I can borrow.
Woodrow Wilson

A successful team is a group of many hands but of one mind.
Bill Bethel

You will find men who want to be carried on the shoulders of others, who think that the world owes them a living. They don't seem to see that we must all lift together and pull together.
Henry Ford

Appreciate everything your associates do for the business. Nothing else can quite substitute for a few well-chosen, well-timed, sincere words of praise. They're absolutely free and worth a fortune.
Sam Walton

When building a team, I always search first for people who love to win. If I can't find any of those, I look for people who hate to lose.
H. Ross Perot

A boss creates fear, a leader confidence. A boss fixes blame, a leader corrects mistakes. A boss knows all, a leader asks questions. A boss makes work drudgery, a leader makes it interesting. A boss is interested in himself or herself, a leader is interested in the group.
Russell H. Ewing

There's nothing greater in the world than when somebody on the team does something good, and everybody gathers around to pat him on the back.
Billy Martin

Individual glory is insignificant when compared to achieving victory as a team.
Dot Richardson

Strength lies in differences, not in similarities.
Stephen R. Covey

Alone we can do so little; together we can do so much.
Helen Keller

Coming together is a beginning; keeping together is progress; working together is success.
Henry Ford

When the best leader's work is done, the people say, "We did it ourselves."
Lao Tzu

You can make more friends in two months by becoming interested in other people than you can in two years by trying to get other people interested in you.
Dale Carnegie

People have been known to achieve more as a result of working with others than against them.
Dr. Allan Fromme

If a team is to reach its potential, each player must be willing to subordinate his personal goals to the good of the team.
Bud Wilkinson

When your team is winning, be ready to be tough, because winning can make you soft. On the other hand, when you team is losing, stick by them. Keep believing.
Bo Schembechler

The way a team plays as a whole determines its success. You may have the greatest bunch of individual stars in the world, but if they don't play together, the club won't be worth a dime.
Babe Ruth

In order to become a leading home run hitter, a batter must be surrounded by good hitters, otherwise, the pitchers will 'pitch around' him. Likewise, many successful people became that way from being on a good team.
Laing Burns Jr.

Teamwork is neither good nor desirable. It is a fact. Wherever people work together or play together they do so as a team. Which team to use for what purpose is a crucial, difficult and risky decision that is even harder to unmake. Managements have yet to learn how to make it.
Peter Drucker

Finding good players is easy. Getting them to play as a team is another story.
Casey Stengel

Many of us are more capable than some of us . . . but none of us is as capable as all of us!!
Tom Wilson

Lots of people want to ride with you in the limo, but what you want is someone who will take the bus with you when the limo breaks down.
Oprah Winfrey

Chapter 13

Confidence

Give us the tools, and we will finish the job.
Winston Churchill

Absolute identity with one's cause is the first and great condition of successful leadership.
Woodrow Wilson

If you focus on winning and attaining, you will win and attain.
Brian Tracy

You can do what you think you can do and you cannot do what you think you cannot do.
Ben Stein

The mind is the limit. As long as the mind can envision the fact that you can do something, you can do it, as long as you really believe 100 percent.
Arnold Schwarzenegger

You are the fruit of the thoughts you have planted and nourished. If you want a better harvest, you must plant better thoughts.
Robert Allen

My philosophy of life is that if we make up our mind what we are going to make of our lives, then work hard toward that goal, we never lose - somehow we win out.
Ronald Reagan

Confidence is contagious. So is lack of confidence.
Michael O'Brien

Don't waste life in doubts and fears; spend yourself on the work before you, well assured that the right performance of this hour's duties will be the best preparation for the hours or ages that follow it.
Ralph Waldo Emerson

Chapter 14

Decisiveness

Abraham Lincoln did not go to Gettysburg having commissioned a poll to find out what would sell in Gettysburg. There were no people with percentages for him, cautioning him about this group or that group or what they found in exit polls a year earlier. When will we have the courage of Lincoln?
Robert Coles

Be willing to make decisions. That's the most important quality in a good leader. Don't fall victim to what I call the ready-aim-aim-aim-aim syndrome. You must be willing to fire.
T. Boone Pickens

The right man is the one who seizes the moment.
Johann Wolfgang von Goethe

Their comes a moment when you have to stop revving up the car and shove it into gear.
David Mahoney

I would rather regret the things I have done than the things I have not.
Lucille Ball

If there is a trait which does characterize leaders it is opportunism. Successful people are very often those who steadfastly refuse to be daunted by disadvantage and have the ability to turn disadvantage to good effect. They are people who seize opportunity and take risks. Leadership then seems to be a matter of personality and character.
John Viney

Luck comes to a man who puts himself in the way of it. You went where something might be found and you found something, simple as that.
Louis L'Amour

Eagles don't flock.
Ross Perot

A good plan implemented today is better than a perfect plan implemented tomorrow.
George Patton

Things may come to those who wait, but only things left by those who hustle.
Abraham Lincoln

What we think or what we know or what we believe is, in the end, of little consequence, The only consequence is what we do.
John Ruskin

Even if you're on the right track you'll get run over if you just sit there.
Will Rogers

An idea is worthless unless you use it.
John C. Maxwell

Destiny is not a matter of chance, it is a matter of choice; it is not a thing to be waited for, it is a thing to be achieved.
William Jennings Bryan

No idea is so outlandish that it should not be considered with a searching but at the same time a steady eye.
Winston Churchill

If your ship doesn't come in, swim out to meet it.
Jonathan Winters

You can't cross a sea by merely staring into the water.
Rabindranath Tagore

Anything worth doing is worth doing now!
Ralph Stayer

If opportunity doesn't knock - build a door.
Milton Berle

You don't drown by falling in the water; you drown by staying there.
Edwin Louis Cole

Everything you want is just outside your comfort zone.
Robert Allen

You have to recognize that every 'out front' maneuver you make is going to be lonely, but if you feel entirely comfortable, then you're not far enough ahead to do any good. That warm sense of everything going well is usually the body temperature at the center of the herd.
John Masters

If I had to sum up in a word what makes a good manager, I'd say decisiveness. You can use the fanciest computers to gather the numbers, but in the end you have to set a timetable and act.
Lee Iacocca

One thing is sure. We have to do something. We have to do the best we know how at the moment . . . ; If it doesn't turn out right, we can modify it as we go along.
Franklin D. Roosevelt

Leaders are problem solvers by talent and temperament, and by choice.
Harlan Cleveland

Again and again, the impossible decision is solved when we see that the problem is only a tough decision waiting to be made.
Robert Schuller

Problems are only opportunities in work clothes.
Henri Kaiser

Uncertainty can lead to paralysis. And if you become indecisive you're dead...
Jim Citrin

Difficulties are opportunities to better things.
Brian Adams

The most serious mistakes are not being made as a result of wrong answers. The truly dangerous thing is asking the wrong questions.
Peter Drucker

Success seems to be connected with action. Successful people keep moving. They make mistakes, but they don't quit.
Conrad Hilton

You can't build a strong corporation with a lot of committees and a board that has to be consulted every turn. You have to be able to make decisions on your own.
Rupert Murdoch

I am certainly not one of those who need to be prodded. In fact, if anything, I am the prod.
Winston Churchill

Be willing to make decisions. That's the most important quality in a good leader.
General George Patton

If you wait to do everything until you're sure it's right, you'll probably never do much of anything.
Win Borden

Don't wait. The time will never be just right.
Napoleon Hill

One of these days is just a day of the weak.
Greg Hickman

Things may come to those who wait, but only the things left by those who hustle.
Abraham Lincoln

The wise does at once what the fool does at last.
Baltasar Gracian

It doesn't matter which side of the fence you get off on sometimes. What matters most is getting off. You cannot make progress without making decisions.
Jim Rohn

The truth is that many people set rules to keep from making decisions.
Mike Krzyzewski

It's not hard to make decisions when you know what your values are.
Roy Disney

The first one gets the oyster the second gets the shell.
Andrew Carnegie

There is a danger in the word someday when what it means is "not this day."
David A. Bednar

Getting an idea should be like sitting on a pin: it should make you jump up and do something.
E. L. Simpson

Everyone who has ever taken a shower has an idea. It's the person who gets out of the shower, dries off, and does something about it that makes a difference.
Nolan Bushnell

Work is the process by which dreams become reality. It is the process by which idle visions become dynamic achievements.
Gordon B. Hinckley

Ideas not coupled with action never become bigger than the brain cells they occupied.
Arnold Glasgow

Your big opportunity may be right where you are now.
Napoleon Hill

It still holds true that man is most uniquely human when he turns obstacles into opportunities.
Eric Hoffer

He who refuses to embrace a unique opportunity loses the prize as surely as if he had failed.
William James

To improve the golden moment of opportunity and catch the good that is within our reach is the great art of life.
Samuel Johnson

Decision and determination are the engineer and fireman of our train to opportunity and success.
Burt Lawlor

I believe that you tend to create your own blessings. You have to prepare yourself so that when opportunity comes, you're ready.

Oprah Winfrey

If a window of opportunity appears, don't pull down the shade.

Tom Peters

Chapter 15

Determination

I know of no easy formula to success. Persist, persist, PERSIST; work, work, WORK—is what counts in the battle of life.
Heber J. Grant

Let us not be content to wait and see what will happen, but give us the determination to make the right things happen.
Peter Marshall

Champions aren't made in the gyms. Champions are made from something they have deep inside them--a desire, a dream, a vision.
Muhammad Ali

Realize that if you have time to whine and complain about something then you have the time to do something about it.
Anthony D'Angelo

Be patient with yourself. Self-growth is tender; it's holy ground. There's no greater investment.
Stephen R. Covey

Talent is cheaper than table salt. What separates the talented individual from the successful one is a lot of hard work.
Stephen King

It may be all it takes to get ahead in the world, but you're not going to get very far without hard work.
Michael Angier

There's no payoff to worry. If you're worried about something you can change, then invest your energy doing something about it.
Michael Angier

Life consists not of a series of circumstances but of a series of choices.
David DeFord

One of the greatest values…is the virtue of honest work. Knowledge without labor is profitless. Knowledge with labor is genius.
Gordon B. Hinckley

Diligence is the mother of good luck.
Benjamin Franklin

The most practical, beautiful, workable philosophy in the world won't work—if you won't.
Zig Ziglar

When we do more than we are paid to do, eventually we will be paid more for what we do.
Zig Ziglar

It is our individual performances, no matter how humble our place in life may be, that will in the long run determine how well ordered the world may become.
Paul C. Packer

Be fanatics. When it comes to being and doing and dreaming the best, be maniacs.
A.M. Rosenthal

The man who does not take pride in his own performance performs nothing in which to take pride.
Thomas J. Watson

Work is the miracle by which talent is brought to the surface and dreams become reality.
Gordon B. Hinckley

Chapter 16

Excellence

Excellence is not an accomplishment. It is a spirit, a never-ending process.
Lawrence M. Miller

The quality of a person's life is in direct proportion to their commitment to excellence, regardless of their chosen field of endeavor.
Vince Lombardi

Quality has to be caused, not controlled.
Philip Crosby

Leadership is the challenge to be something more than average.
Jim Rohn

Ability is what you're capable of doing. Motivation determines what you do. Attitude determines how well you do it.
Lou Holtz

Good leadership consists of showing average people how to do the work of superior people.
John D. Rockefeller

Leadership is unlocking people's potential to become better.
Bill Bradley

If you refuse to accept anything but the best, you very often get it.
W. Somerset Maugham

Excellence always sells.
Earl Nightingale

Excellence is not a skill. It is an attitude.
Ralph Marston

Strive for excellence, not perfection.
H. Jackson Brown Jr.

If you want to achieve excellence, you can get there today. As of this second, quit doing less-than-excellent work.
Thomas J. Watson

People think that at the top there isn't much room. They tend to think of it as an Everest. My message is that there is tons of room at the top.
Margaret Thatcher

Excellence is the gradual result of always striving to do better.
Pat Riley

Paint a masterpiece daily. Always autograph your work with excellence.
Greg Hickman

Always do your best. What you plant now, you will harvest later.
Og Mandino

Hold yourself responsible for a higher standard than anybody expects of you. Never excuse yourself.
Henry Ward Beecher

The roots of true achievement lie in the will to become the best that you can become.
Harold Taylor

It's never crowded along the extra mile.
Dr. Wayne Dyer

Circumstance plays a minor role in the outcome of our lives. Our choices determine the paths we take.
David DeFord

My philosophy is that not only are you responsible for your life but doing the best at this moment puts you in the best place for the next moment.
Oprah Winfrey

If you are going to achieve excellence in big things, you develop the habit in little matters. Excellence is not an exception, it is a prevailing attitude.
Colin Powell

Always keep good company. Never waste an hour with anyone who doesn't lift you up and encourage you.
Spencer W. Kimball

Not to go out and do your best is to sacrifice the gift.
Steve Prefontaine

Life is a competition not with others, but with ourselves. We should seek each day to live stronger, better, truer lives; each day to master some weakness of yesterday; each day to repair a mistake; each day to surpass ourselves.
David B. Haight

In God's eyes, nobody is a nobody. We should never lose sight of what we may become and who we are.
Marvin J. Ashton

Perform every act in life as though it were your last.
Marcus Aurelius

Keep away from people who try to belittle your ambitions. Small people always do that, but the really great make you feel that you, too, can become great.
Mark Twain

I strive to improve my writing by making it active. I strive to improve my life in the same way.
David DeFord

Great works are performed, not by strength, but by perseverance.
Samuel Johnson

The accumulation of many well-made small choices has the same impact as the sprinkling of a few tiny drops of cayenne pepper sauce—tremendous power!
David DeFord

Major improvements follow minor adjustments.
David DeFord

You can't hope for the best. You have to do the best.
Dusty Baker

The person who is waiting for something to turn up might start with their shirt sleeves.
Garth Henrichs

The minute you settle for less than you deserve, you get even less than you settled for.
Maureen Dowd

Excellence is not a destination; it is a continuous journey that never ends.
Brian Tracy

Leadership is the challenge to be something more than average.
Jim Rohn

Since most of us spend our lives doing ordinary tasks, the most important thing is to carry them out extraordinarily well.
Henry David Thoreau

He should sweep streets so well that all the host of heaven and earth will pause to say, 'Here lives a great street-sweeper who did his job well'.
Martin Luther King Jr.

Management is doing things right; leadership is doing the right things.
Peter Drucker

The leadership instinct you are born with is the backbone. You develop the funny bone and the wishbone that go with it.
Elaine Agather

Most of what we call management consists of making it difficult for people to get their jobs done.
Peter Drucker

A competent leader can get efficient service from poor troops, while on the contrary an incapable leader can demoralize the best of troops.
General John J. Pershing

Processes don't do work, people do.
John Seely Brown

Leadership is practiced not so much in words as in attitude and in actions.
Harold Geneen

The task of the leader is to get his people from where they are to where they have not been.
Henry Kissinger

Whoever is providing leadership needs to be as fresh and thoughtful and reflective as possible to make the very best fight.
Faye Wattleton

Management is efficiency in climbing the ladder of success; leadership determines whether the ladder is leaning against the right wall.
Stephen R. Covey

The older I get the less I listen to what people say and the more I look at what they do.
Andrew Carnegie

I think that the best training a top manager can be engaged in is management by example.
Carlos Ghosn

Effective leadership is not about making speeches or being liked; leadership is defined by results not attributes.
Peter Drucker

When the leadership is right and the time is right, the people can always be counted upon to follow—to the end and at all costs.
Harold J. Seymour

A true leader always keeps an element of surprise up his sleeve, which others cannot grasp but which keeps his public excited and breathless.
Charles deGaulle

Leadership is getting someone to do what they don't want to do, to achieve what they want to achieve.
Tom Landry

Great necessities call forth great leaders.
Abigail Adams

Leadership is much more an art, a belief, a condition of the heart, than a set of things to do. The visible signs of artful leadership are expressed, ultimately, in its practice.
Max DePree

No organization is stronger than the quality of its leadership, or ever extends its constituency far beyond the degree to which its leadership is representative.
Edgar Powell

Leadership is the special quality that enables people to stand up and pull the rest of us over the horizon.
James L. Fisher

Leaders don't force people to follow—they invite them on a journey.
Charles S. Lauer

Leadership is understanding people and involving them to help you do a job. That takes all of the good characteristics, like integrity, dedication of purpose, selflessness, knowledge, skill, implacability, as well as determination not to accept failure.
Admiral Arleigh A. Burke

The question, 'Who ought to be boss?', is like asking, 'Who ought to be the tenor in the quartet?' Obviously, the man who can sing tenor.
Henry Ford

Charisma becomes the undoing of leaders. It makes them inflexible, convinced of their own infallibility, unable to change.
Peter Drucker

Whoever is providing leadership needs to be as fresh and thoughtful and reflective as possible to make the very best fight.
Faye Wattleton

Forget about style; worry about results.
Bobby Orr

There is no such thing as failure. There are only results.
Anthony Robbins

You can't build a reputation on what you are going to do.
Henry Ford

The achievements of an organization are the results of the combined effort of each individual.
Vincent Lombardi

You always succeed in producing a result.
Anthony Robbins

Big results require big ambitions.
James Champy

One of the true tests of leadership is the ability to recognize a problem before it becomes an emergency.
Arnold Glasgow

There is nothing in all the world so satisfying as a task well done. There is no reward so pleasing as that which comes with the mastery of a difficult problem.
Gordon B. Hinckley

You have to perform at a consistently higher level than others. That's the mark of a true professional.
Joe Paterno

The major work of the world is not done by geniuses. It is done by ordinary people, with balance in their lives, who have learned to work in an extraordinary manner.
Gordon B. Hinckley

The talent of success is nothing more than doing what you can do well, and doing well whatever you do...
Henry W. Longfellow

There are important cases in which the difference between half a heart and a whole heart makes just the difference between signal defeat and a splendid victory.
A. H. K. Boyd

Men talk as if victory were something fortunate. Work is victory.
Ralph Waldo Emerson

The ultimate victory in competition is derived from the inner satisfaction of knowing that you have done your best and that you have gotten the most out of what you had to give.
Howard Cosell

I would rather lose in a cause that will some day win, than win in a cause that will some day lose!
Woodrow Wilson

Accept the challenges, so that you may feel the exhilaration of victory.
General George Patton

It is not enough to fight. It is the spirit which we bring to the fight that decides the issue. It is morale that wins the victory.
General George Marshall

Far better it is to dare mighty things, to win glorious triumphs, even though checkered by failure, than to take rank with those poor spirits who neither enjoy much nor suffer much, because they live in the grey twilight that knows not victory nor defeat.
Theodore Roosevelt

Chapter 17

Focus

The human mind is not rich enough to drive many horses abreast and wants one general scheme, under which it strives to bring everything.
George Santayana

The successful woman is the average woman--focused.
Ruth Williams

Nothing focuses the mind better than the constant sight of a competitor who wants to wipe you off the map.
Wayne Calloway

There are two ways to look at life and the world. We can see the good or the bad, the beautiful or the ugly. Both are there, and what we focus on and choose to see is what brings us feelings of joy or feelings of despair.
Lloyd Newell

Most people have no idea of the giant capacity we can immediately command when we focus all of our resources on mastering a single area of our lives.
Anthony Robbins

If you focus on results, you will never change. If you focus on change, you will get results.
Jack Dixon

It's not what's happening to you now or what has happened in your past that determines who you become. Rather, it's your decisions about what to focus on, what things mean to you, and what you're going to do about them that will determine your ultimate destiny.
Anthony Robbins

The successful warrior is the average man, with laser-like focus.
Bruce Lee

Do not let what you can't do interfere with what you can do.
John Wooden

Keep your mind on the things you want and off the things you don't want.
Hannah Whitall Smith

Chapter 18

Growth and Learning

There is no such thing as a perfect leader either in the past or present, in China or elsewhere. If there is one, he is only pretending, like a pig inserting scallions into its nose in an effort to look like an elephant.
Liu Shao-ch'i

Life is change. Growth is optional. Choose wisely.
Karen Kaiser Clark

The only real training for leadership is leadership.
Anthony Jay

In times of change, learners inherit the Earth, while the learned find themselves beautifully equipped to deal with a world that no longer exists.
Eric Hoffer

Leaders are more powerful role models when they learn than when they teach.
Rosabeth Moss Kantor

Leadership cannot really be taught. It can only be learned.
Harold Geneen

Leaders aren't born they are made. And they are made just like anything else, through hard work. And that's the price we'll have to pay to achieve that goal, or any goal.

Vince Lombardi

The most dangerous leadership myth is that leaders are born -- that there is a genetic factor to leadership. This myth asserts that people simply either have certain charismatic qualities or not. That's nonsense; in fact, the opposite is true. Leaders are made rather than born.

Warren Bennis

Before you are a leader, success is all about growing yourself. When you become a leader, success is all about growing others.

Jack Welch

One key to successful leadership is continuous personal change. Personal change is a reflection of our inner growth and empowerment.

Robert E. Quinn

The measure of success is not whether you have a tough problem to deal with, but whether it is the same problem you had last year.

John Foster Dulles

The majority see the obstacles; the few see the objectives; history records the successes of the latter, while oblivion is the reward of the former.

Alfred Armand Montapert

Leadership and learning are indispensable to each other.
John F. Kennedy

One quality of leaders and high achievers in every area seems to be a commitment to ongoing personal and professional development.
Brian Tracy

Leadership is not something that you learn once and for all. It is an ever-evolving pattern of skills, talents, and ideas that grow and change as you do.
Sheila Murray Bethel

An ability to embrace new ideas, routinely challenge old ones, and live with paradox will be the effective leader's premier trait.
Tom Peters

In times of change, learners inherit the Earth, while the learned find themselves beautifully equipped to deal with a world that no longer exists.
Eric Hoffer

What has become clear over the years is that a "best" leadership style does not exist; rather a successful leader is one that matches the style with the current situation to maximize productivity and human satisfaction. The adaptability of a leader appears to be his or her greatest asset.
Anne Breen

He who moves not forward, goes backward.
Johann Wolfgang von Goethe

If I accept you as you are, I will make you worse; however if I treat you as though you are what you are capable of becoming, I help you become that.
Johann Wolfgang von Goethe

Natural abilities are like natural plants; they need pruning by study.
Francis Bacon

The man who views the world at 50 the same as he did at 20 has wasted 30 years of his life.
Muhammad Ali

Contrary to the old saying that leaders are born not made, the art of leading can be taught and it can be mastered.
General Mark W. Clark

Apply yourself. Get all the education you can, but then, by God, do something. Don't just stand there, make something happen.
Lee Iacocca

Chapter 19

Persuasion and Communication

Leadership in today's world requires far more than a large stock of gunboats and a hard fist at the conference table.
Hubert H. Humphrey

People ask the difference between a leader and a boss. . . . The leader works in the open, and the boss in covert. The leader leads, and the boss drives.
Theodore Roosevelt

There is no contest between the company that buys the grudging compliance of its work force and the company that enjoys the enterprising participation of its employees
Ricardo Sempler

Understanding human needs is half the job of meeting them.
Adlai Stevenson

Lead and inspire people. Don't try to manage and manipulate people. Inventories can be managed but people must be lead.
Ross Perot

Leadership is understanding people and involving them to help you do a job. That takes all of the good characteristics, like integrity, dedication of purpose, selflessness, knowledge, skill, implacability, as well as determination not to accept failure.
Admiral Arleigh A. Burke

People are more easily led than driven.
David Harold Fink

The art of leading, in operations large or small, is the art of dealing with humanity, of working diligently on behalf of men, of being sympathetic with them, but equally, of insisting that they make a square facing toward their own problems.
S. L. A. Marshall

You do not lead by hitting people over the head - that's assault, not leadership.
Dwight D. Eisenhower

Leadership is not manifested by coercion, even against the resented.
Margaret Chase Smith

The leaders who work most effectively, it seems to me, never say "I."
Peter Drucker

A leader takes people where they want to go. A great leader takes people where they don't necessarily want to go, but ought to be.
Rosalynn Carter

If the blind lead the blind, both shall fall in the ditch.
Jesus Christ

Control is not leadership.
Dee Hock

Never give an order that can't be obeyed.
General Douglas MacArthur

Great leaders are almost always great simplifiers, who can cut through argument, debate, and doubt to offer a solution everybody can understand.
General Colin Powell

All leadership is influence.
John C. Maxwell

Your position never gives you the right to command. It only imposes on you the duty of so living your life that others may receive your orders without being humiliated.
Dag Hammarskjöld

He who has great power should use it lightly.
Seneca

You don't lead by pointing and telling people some place to go. You lead by going to that place and making a case.
Ken Kesey

Leadership is the ability to establish standards and manage a creative climate where people are self-motivated toward the mastery of long term constructive goals, in a participatory environment of mutual respect, compatible with personal values.
Mike Vance

In the modern world of business it is useless to be a creative original thinker unless you can also sell what you create. Management cannot be expected to recognize a good idea unless it is presented to them by a good salesman.
David M. Ogilvy

If a leader can't get a message across clearly and motivate others to act on it, then having a message doesn't even matter.
Gilbert Amelio

Communicate downward to subordinates with at least the same care and attention as you communicate upward to superiors.
L. B. Belker

Regardless of the changes in technology, the market for well-crafted messages will always have an audience.
Steve Burnett

You can have brilliant ideas, but if you can't get them across, your ideas won't get you anywhere.
Lee Iacocca

A sense of humor can be a great help—particularly a sense of humor about (oneself). William Howard Taft joked about his own corpulence and people loved it; took nothing from his inherent dignity. Lincoln eased tense moments with bawdy stories, and often poked fun at himself—and history honors him for this human quality. A sense of humor is part of the art of leadership, of getting along with people, of getting things done.
Dwight D. Eisenhower

Be amusing: never tell unkind stories; above all, never tell long ones.
Benjamin Disraeli

Communicate unto the other person that which you would want him to communicate unto you if your positions were reversed.
Aaron Goldman

The art of communication is the language of leadership.
James Humes

In everyone's life, at some time, our inner fire goes out. It is then burst into flame by an encounter with another human being. We should all be thankful for those people who rekindle the inner spirit.
Albert Schweitzer

Leadership is the activity of influencing people to cooperate toward some goal which they come to find desirable.
Ordway Tead

Any business or industry that pays equal rewards to its goof-off and its eager beavers sooner or later will find itself with more goof-offs than eager beavers.
Mick Delaney

In motivating people, you've got to engage their minds and their hearts. It is good business to have an employee feel part of the entire effort . . . ; I motivate people, I hope, by example—and perhaps by excitement, by having provocative ideas to make others feel involved.
Rupert Murdoch

Good executives never put off until tomorrow what they can get someone else to do today.
John C. Maxwell

Educators take something simple and make it complicated. Communicators take something complicated and make it simple.
John C. Maxwell

A good objective of leadership is to help those who are doing poorly to do well and to help those who are doing well to do even better.
Jim Rohn

Pull the string, and it will follow wherever you wish. Push it, and it will go nowhere at all.
Dwight D. Eisenhower

A man who wants to lead the orchestra must turn his back on the crowd.
Max Lucado

Treat people as if they were what they ought to be and you help them to become what they are capable of being.
Johann Wolfgang Von Goethe

I am looking for a lot of men who have an infinite capacity to not know what can't be done.
Henry Ford

Skill in the art of communication is crucial to a leader's success. He can accomplish nothing unless he can communicate effectively.
Norman Allen

Leadership is the wise use of power. Power is the capacity to translate intention into reality and sustain it.
Warren Bennis

Example has more followers than reason. We unconsciously imitate what pleases us, and approximate to the characters we most admire.
Christian Nevell Bovee

I have yet to find a man, however exalted his station, who did not do better work and put forth greater effort under a spirit of approval than under a spirit of criticism.

Charles Schwab

Outstanding leaders go out of their way to boost the self-esteem of their personnel. If people believe in themselves, it's amazing what they can accomplish.

Sam Walton

The pessimist complains about the wind. The optimist expects it to change. The leader adjusts the sails.

John C. Maxwell

People don't care how much you know--until they know how much you care.

John C. Maxwell

Leadership is all about people. It is not about organizations. It is not about plans. It is not about strategies. It is all about people--motivating people to get the job done. You have to be people-centered.

Colin Powell

Trust is the essence of leadership.

Colin Powell

As we look ahead into the next century, leaders will be those who empower others.

Bill Gates

The difference between a boss and a leader: a boss says, 'Go!' -a leader says, 'Let's go!'

M. Kelly

Dictators are rulers who always look good until the last ten minutes.

Jan Masaryk

The key to successful leadership today is influence, not authority.

Ken Blanchard

Perhaps the most central characteristic of authentic leadership is the relinquishing of the impulse to dominate others.

David Cooper

Leadership is getting people to help you when they are not obligated to do so.

John C. Maxwell

Managers control. Leaders create commitment.

John Zenger

The world is moved not only by the mighty shoves of the heroes, but also by the aggregate of the tiny pushes of each honest worker.

Frank C. Ross

If you really want people to respond to your leadership, you have to have a personal relationship with them. They need to know you're dependable and that you'll be there if they have a problem. That's personal power to me.

Noreen Haffner

The leadership instinct you are born with is the backbone. You develop the funny bone and the wishbone that go with it.

Elaine Agather

In organizations, real power and energy is generated through relationships. The patterns of relationships and the capacities to form them are more important than tasks, functions, roles, and positions.
Margaret Wheatley

Power wielders may treat people as things. Leaders may not.
James MacGregor Burns

In the past a leader was a boss. Today's leaders must be partners with their people.. they no longer can lead solely based on positional power.
Ken Blanchard

The key to being a good manager is keeping the people who hate me away from those who are still undecided.
Casey Stengel

We can never pay people enough to care – to care about their products, services, communities, or families, or even the bottom line. True leaders tap into people's hearts and minds, not merely their hands and wallets.
James M. Kouzes and Barry Z. Posner

It's your job as leader to create an atmosphere that... transforms antagonism into creative energy.
John Kao

Some people change when they see the light, others when they feel the heat.

Leaders need to foster environments and work processes within which people can develop high-quality relationships— relationships with each other, relationships with the group with which we work, relationships with our clients and customers.
Max Dupree

A competent leader can get efficient service from poor troops, while on the contrary an incapable leader can demoralize the best of troops.
General John J. Pershing

Processes don't do work, people do.
John Seely Brown

Kind words can be short and easy to speak, but their echoes are truly endless.
Mother Teresa

Speech is power: speech is to persuade, to convert, to compel. It is to bring another out of his bad sense into your good sense.
Ralph Waldo Emerson

Kind words do not cost much. Yet they accomplish much.
Blaise Pascal

They may forget what you said, but they will never forget how you made them feel.
Carl W. Buechner

You cannot raise a man up by calling him down.
William Boetcker

When dealing with people, remember you are not dealing with creatures of logic, but creatures of emotion.
Dale Carnegie

Note how good you feel after you have encouraged someone else. No other argument is necessary to suggest that never miss the opportunity to give encouragement.
George Adams

You need to be aware of what others are doing, applaud their efforts, acknowledge their successes, and encourage them in their pursuits. When we all help one another, everybody wins.
Jim Stovall

Appreciation can make a day - even change a life, Your willingness to put it into words is all that is necessary.
Margaret Cousins

Those who are lifting the world upward and onward are those who encourage more than criticize.
Elizabeth Harrison

Correction does much, but encouragement does more. Encouragement after censure is as the sun after a shower.
Johann Wolfgang von Goethe

Enthusiasm is the yeast that makes your hopes shine to the stars. Enthusiasm is the sparkle in your eyes, the swing in your gait. The grip of your hand, the irresistible surge of will and energy to execute your ideas.
Henry Ford

Celebrate what you want to see more of.
Tom Peters

Nothing is more effective than sincere, accurate praise, and nothing is more lame than a cookie-cutter compliment.
Bill Walsh

There is only one way to get anybody to do anything. And that is by making the other person want to do it.
Dale Carnegie

No matter how busy you are, you must take time to make the other person feel important.
Mary Kay Ash

A pat on the back is only a few vertebrae removed from a kick in the pants, but is miles ahead in results.
Ella Wheeler Wilcox

I do believe in praising that which deserves to be praised.
Dean Smith

I have yet to find the man, however exalted his station, who did not do better work and put forth greater effort under a spirit of approval than under a spirit of criticism.
Charles Schwab

We increase whatever we praise. The whole creation responds to praise, and is glad.
Charles Fillmore

Few things in the world are more powerful than a positive push. A smile. A world of optimism and hope. A "you can do it" when things are tough.
Richard M. DeVos

There is no investment you can make which will pay you so well as the effort to scatter sunshine and good cheer through your establishment.
Orison Swett Marden

Everyone has an invisible sign hanging from their neck saying, "Make me feel important." Never forget this message when working with people.
Mary Kay Ash

Appreciative words are the most powerful force for good on earth!
George W. Crane

I can live for two months on a good compliment.
Mark Twain

Respect a man, and he will do all the more.
John Wooden

Every human being, of whatever origin, of whatever station, deserves respect. We must each respect others even as we respect ourselves.
U Thant

If you have some respect for people as they are, you can be more effective in helping them to become better than they are.
John W. Gardner

I must respect the opinions of others even if I disagree with them.
Herbert Henry Lehman

Always treat your employees exactly as you want them to treat your best customers.
Stephen R. Covey

Chapter 20

Planning and Preparation

Unless commitment is made, there are only promises and hopes... but no plans.
Peter Drucker

Good plans shape good decisions. That's why good planning helps to make elusive dreams come true.
Lester R. Bittel

No institution can possibly survive if it needs geniuses or supermen to manage it. It must be organized in such a way as to be able to get along under a leadership composed of average human beings.
Peter Drucker

It's not the will to win, but the will to prepare to win that makes the difference.
Paul "Bear" Bryant

Setting a goal is not the main thing. It is deciding how you will go about achieving it and staying with that plan.
Tom Landry

Before beginning, plan carefully.
Marcus T. Cicero

It takes as much energy to wish as it does to plan.
Eleanor Roosevelt

A good plan today is better than a perfect plan tomorrow.
George Patton

Reduce your plan to writing. The moment you complete this, you will have definitely given concrete form to the intangible desire.
Napoleon Hill

I find it fascinating that most people plan their vacations with better care than they plan their lives. Perhaps that is because escape is easier than change.
Jim Rohn

The meeting of preparation with opportunity generates the offspring we call luck.
Anthony Robbins

Sources

Angier, Michael E., *101 Best Ways to Be Your Best: Practical Wisdom to Help You Maximize Your Unique Potential.* South Burlington, VT: Success Networks International, Inc., 2005.

Enberg, Dick, *Dick Enberg's Humorous Quotes for All Occasions.* Kansas City, MO: Andrews McMeel Universal, 2000.

Humes, James C., *The Sir Winston Method: The Five Secrets of Speaking the Language of Leadership.* New York: William Morrow and Company, Inc., 1991.

Maxwell, James C., *The 21 Irrefutable Laws of Leadership.* Atlanta: Maxwell Motivation, Inc., 1998.

Maxwell, James C., *Developing the Leader Within You.* Atlanta: Injoy, Inc., 1993.

Maxwell, James C., *The 17 Indisputable Laws of Teamwork.* Atlanta: Maxwell Motivation, Inc., 2001.

Phillips, Bob, *Phillips' Book of Great Thoughts & Funny Sayings.* Wheaton, IL: Tyndale House Publishers, Inc., 1993.

Rubin, Louis D. Jr., *The Quotable Baseball Fanatic.* New York: The Lyons Press, 2000.

Tripp, Rhoda Thomas, *The International Thesaurus of Quotations*. New York: Harper & Row, Publishers, Inc., 1970.

www.ingramcontent.com/pod-product-compliance
Lightning Source LLC
Chambersburg PA
CBHW052258220526
45471CB00001B/394